G000110169

living &

working

IN FRANCE

1st edition

Charles Davey

TEE FRANCE

STANLEY TEE

Bishop's Stortford
England

Published in 2006 by Tee France,
Stanley Tee,
High Street,
Bishop's Stortford,
Hertfordshire, CM23 2LU
England
www.teefrance.co.uk
www.stanleytee.co.uk

This book is for general information and guidance only. No legal responsibility can be accepted by the author or publishers for the accuracy of the contents of the book, nor for any loss or expense resulting from reliance upon it. Readers should always obtain specific up-to-date advice from a lawyer or other appropriately qualified expert before committing themselves.

All rights reserved. No part of this publication may be reproduced, stored in a retrieval system, or transmitted in any form or by any means without the prior permission of Stanley Tee, save for fair dealing for the carrying out of research, private study, review or criticism as permitted under The Copyright, Design and Patents Act 1988.

Copyright © Charles Davey & Stanley Tee 2006

ISBN 0-9552442-0-X
978-0-9552442-0-9

Designed and Produced by Royston Simpson Creative,
16 Church Street, Bishop's Stortford,
Hertfordshire, CM23 2LY,
England
www.roystonsimpson.co.uk

Printed by Ian Douglas, Design and Print,
9 Raynham Close, Raynham Road Industrial Estate,
Bishop's Stortford, Hertfordshire, CM23 5JP,
England
www.iddp.co.uk

CONTENTS

PREFACE

The last ten years have seen a dramatic rise in cross-cultural exchanges between France and the UK. There are now an estimated 300, 000 French citizens working in the UK, with a similar number of Britons having made the move to France. According to the British Embassy, there are an estimated 500,000 British citizens who now own property across the Channel. Whilst in the past British purchasers were looking for holiday or retirement homes, many are now intending to settle in France, with estate agents reporting a substantial increase in the number of purchasers aged 35-44.

The last decade has witnessed an extraordinary increase in air travel, which has been particularly steep in the last three years or so. It is now possible to fly direct to destinations in France from provincial airports across the UK, with the more recent developments including the routes from Coventry, the new Doncaster/Sheffield airport, Durham Tees Valley, Edinburgh, Glasgow, Leeds/Bradford and Manchester.

2004/5 saw a notable improvement in air links with Brittany, with the launch of flights to Brest from Birmingham, Exeter, and Southampton, to Rennes from Southampton, and to Dinard from London Luton, as well as from Galway and Waterford in the Republic of Ireland to Lorient in southern Brittany. This trend is set to continue with Air Arann starting flights from London to Lorient from March 2006.

This unprecedented growth in passenger travel has been accompanied by, and indeed partially fuelled by, increased job mobility across Europe. Following the introduction of European Regulations across a wide range of occupations, the French authorities have been compelled to recognise the qualifications gained in other EU member states. Any citizen of a member state is now permitted to live and work in France. They are entitled to recognition of their professional qualifications, and to continue their occupation in France. The laws of the new Europe are clear: the French authorities are required to treat non-French EU nationals as they would their own citizens. This applies to the provision of guidance and assistance in finding employment, obtaining occupational training and qualifications, and setting up businesses. It embraces also such areas

3

as housing, social security and taxation.

Large numbers of people and businesses are taking advantage of the services of EURES, which provides assistance in relation to job placements for those wishing to work in another EU member state. In addition to practical help and advice available via its web site, EURES also has a team of specialist advisers placed across Europe.

In this book I have sought to set out guidance for those wishing to live and work in France, whether in the short term, or indefinitely, in a clear and concise manner. This is not a book about buying property in France, which I have covered in detail in *The Complete Guide to Buying Property in France* (published by Kogan Page 2005).

Charles Davey

January 2006

ACKNOWLEDGEMENTS

I would like to express my thanks to those at Tee France who have helped this book come to fruition, in particular David Redfern, the managing partner for his initial thoughts, his enthusiasm and support, John Donovan the senior partner for his meticulous attention to detail, and *Maître* Hervé Blatry, Tee France's French avocat, for his advice and assistance most notably in relation to *Les impôt sur les plus-values*. My thanks also go to Cathy Izzard, partner at Tee France and Sarah Blackaby at Royston Simpson Creative in relation to their design of the cover, and Eve Elliott of Royston Simpson Creative for bringing the book together.

Chapter One

THE REGIONS OF FRANCE:
CHOOSING WHERE TO LIVE

France is a large country with a diverse geography and climate. Northern and western France is mostly flat. Along the eastern side are the mountain ranges of the Vosges, Jura and the Alpes that extend to the borders with Germany, Switzerland and Italy. The south eastern corner, bordered by the Rhône to the west (or a line down from Lyon to Marseille), and the Italian border to the east is almost entirely mountainous. Central France is dominated by the Massif Central, another mountainous mass to the west of the Rhone extending almost to Angoulême in the west and almost to Toulouse in the south. Finally the border with Spain is dominated by the Pyrenees, stretching from the Atlantic coast to the Mediterranean. As to its climate, most of northern France and western France boast an oceanic climate, with the sea warming the land in winter, and cooling it in summer. Eastern France, and much of the regions of the mid-Pyrenees and Limousin suffer from a continental climate in which, far from the beneficial effects of the sea, they suffer from stifling hot summers, and extremely cold winters.The Mediterranean, of course, enjoys a separate climatic system, with very mild winters and scorching summers, with the inland mountainous areas remaining cool even during the summer months. As to rainfall, those areas north of the Loire Valley receive significantly higher levels of rainfall than those to the south.

Other factors that are likely to be high on your list are property prices, employment prospects, educational facilities for your children and transport links to the UK. Areas that have low unemployment are seldom the cheapest, and those with a selection of international schools and the best airline links are frequently the most expensive, with Paris and the Riviera obviously falling into this category. As far as property prices are concerned, these are understandably significantly higher in coastal areas.

Administratively France is divided into 22 regions and 95 departments. I have included details relating to each region below, crossing France from west to east, and starting in the north.

Nord-Pas de Calais
59 Nord
62 Pas de Calais

Normandie
27 Eure
76 Seine maritime
14 Calvados
50 Manche
61 Orne

Picardie
02 Aisne
60 Oise
80 Somme

Île de France
75 Ville de Paris
77 Seine et Marne
78 Yvelines
91 Essonne
92 Hauts de Seine
93 Seine-Saint-Denis
94 Val de Marne
95 Val de Oise

Champagne-Ardennes
08 Ardennes
10 Aube
51 Marne
52 Haute Marne

Lorraine
54 Meurthe et Moselle
55 Meuse
57 Mosells
88 Vosges

Alsace
67 Bas Rhin
68 Haut Rhin

Bretagne
22 Côtes d'Armor
29 Finistère
35 Îlle et Vilaine
56 Morbihan
Pays de la Loire
44 Loire Atlantique
49 Maine et Loire

53 Mayenne
72 Sarthe
85 Vendée

Centre
18 Cher
28 Eure et Loire
36 Indre
37 Indre et Loire
41 Loir et Cher
45 Loiret

Bourgogne
21 Côte d'Or
58 Nièvre
71 Saône et Loire
89 Yonne

Franche-Comté
25 Doubs
39 Jura
70 Haute Saône
90 Territoire de Belfont

Poitou-Charentes
16 Charente
17 Charente Maritime
79 Deux Sèvres
86 Vienne

Limousin
19 Corrèze
23 Creuse
87 Haute Vienne

Auvergne
03 Allier
15 Cantal
43 Haute Loire
63 Puy de Dôme

Rhône Alpes
01 Ain
07 Ardeche
26 Drôme
38 Isère
42 Loire
69 Rhône
73 Savoie
74 Haute Savoie

Aquitaine
24 Dordogne
33 Gironde
40 Landes
47 Lot et Garonne
64 Pyrénées Atlantiques

Midi-Pyrénées
09 Ariège
12 Aveyron
31 Haute Garonne
32 Gers
46 Lot
65 Haute Pyrénées
81 Tarn
82 Tarn et Garonne

Languedoc-Roussillon
11 Aude
30 Gard
34 Hérault
48 Lozère
46 Pyrénées Orientales

Provence-Alpes-Côtes d'Azur
04 Alpes de Haute Provence
05 Haute Alpes
06 Alpes Maritimes
13 Bouche du Rhône
83 Var
84 Vaucluse

Corse
20A Corse du Sud
20B Haute Corse

NORD-PAS DE CALAIS

(departments of Nord (59) and Pas de Calais (62))

Historically the links between this region and England date back many centuries, with Calais a possession of the English Crown for over two hundred years from 1347 to 1558, and now a major gateway for British visitors to France. The Channel Tunnel has resulted in the development of many commercial links between Lille and the UK. The European agency EURES has established cross-border partnerships involving both trade unions, employer organisations, regional authorities and vocational training services, covering Kent, Belgium and the North East corner of France. In these areas people often live in one country and work in another. You can obtain extremely helpful advice and assistance from the EURES advisers in relation to the administrative, legal or tax complications that are often encountered on a daily basis (see www.europa.eu.int/eures).

The region's main centre is the city of Lille, which with a population of almost a million, is the fourth largest city in France. This is a region that played a major role in France's industrial growth, and which remains heavily industrialised. Valenciennes is the site of a new Toyota plant and other new businesses. The new town of Villeneuve d'Ascq has benefited from the creation of new jobs in the information technology and communication industries.

The coastline is referred to as *The Opal Coast*, and for the most part remains unspoilt, with long sandy beaches and dunes. The resorts of Le Touquet, Hardelot, and Wimereux have been particularly popular with the British who played a major role in their development from the late Victorian era (for Le Touqet, visit www.letouquet.com). The region has a good selection of golf courses, and centres for horse-riding, sailing and sand yachting. The climate during the winter is cold, and rather like the UK. There is a retirement home at Fort-Mahon (one hour from Calais) at which English is spoken, called *Les Jardins de Cybèle* tel: 04 66 63 21 05 www.jardins-de-cybele.tm.fr .

In Lille, the British Cultural Centre is a meeting place frequented by many English speakers (tel: 0320542279) with a reasonably stocked library. The British Community Association also organises social activities and can be contacted via the British Consulate (03 20 12 82 72). There is an English bookshop in Lille, *Books et Alia*, 10 rue de la Barre, 59000 (tel: 03 20 74 32 67). There is a private day and boarding school just outside Lille, the *Ecole Active Bilingue Jeannine Manuel* (03 20906550). For Anglican church services in Lille, and information on other Anglican churches in the region, contact 03 28 52 66 36.

The journey time from London to Lille via the Channel Tunnel is around two hours. There are ferry services from Dover to Calais, Dunkirk and Boulogne, and a 50 minute catamaran service from Dover to Boulogne. Lille is a major rail centre for journeys across Europe.

There is a small airport at Le Touquet with flights to Brighton (Shoreham airport) with www.euroexec.com (from around £80 return), or to Lydd airport in Kent (see www.lyddair.com).

NORMANDY
(departments of Eure (27), Seine-Maritime (76), Calvados (14), Manche (50) and Orne(61))

La Basse Normandie, that is the departments of Calvados, Manche and Orne, is noted for its rugged landscape. Normandy produces much of France's agricultural output, though today the vast majority of the region's work force is employed in the industrial and service sectors. The ports of Le Havre and Dieppe are extremely busy. Rouen, with its beautiful medieval town centre, is the historic capital of Normandy, and boasts much Gothic and Renaissance architecture (see www.rouentourisme.com). The departments of Eure and Seine-Maritime are regularly visited by Parisians, many of whom have purchased second homes. The resorts of Deauville and Honfleur are particularly popular.

A new website has been launched to help both employers and those seeking work in *Haute Normandie* – www.affaireonline.com. In 2005 the social security authorities in the department of Manche introduced a hotline for English speakers to answer questions concerning social security (tel: 0820 904 212).

Normandy is extremely popular with the British, and large numbers have settled here. The Association France-Grande-Bretagne can offer you advice, assistance and a friendly welcome (tel 02 31 73 18 80). Angloinfo has recently started its Normandy site, www.normandy-angloinfo.com and has much useful information on living in France and in Normandy. Another English speaking site that is well worth visiting is www.ukgrapevine.monsite.wanadoo.fr. Those in search of an English library, or films in English should visit the Franco-American Institute in Rennes (02 99 79 20 57). Though in Brittany, Rennes is easily accessible from southern Normandy and also has an international school. There are English bookshops in Domfront (61), tel: 02 33 37 13 020 and in Rouen (the ABC Bookshop, 11, rue des Faulx, 76000 (tel: 02 35 71 08 67). There are a number of Anglican churches in the region, including at Caen, Rouen, Auxais and Coutances.

Flybe now flies from Southampton to Cherbourg and Rennes, and www.euroexec.com flies from Brighton to Le Havre (from around £80 return). Those living in the east of the region are not far from the Paris

Beauvais airport from which Ryanair operates flights to Glasgow (and also to Dublin, Shannon, Rome, Venice, Stockholm, Milan and Barcelona) There are ferry services from Newhaven, Portsmouth and Poole to the Normandy ports of Dieppe, Cherbourg and Le Havre, most of them operated by P&O or Brittany ferries. There is a high-speed catamaran service operated by P&O between Portsmouth and Caen, with a crossing time of three and a half hours. Paris is an hour and a half from Rouen by train or car, and two hours from Caen by train and two and a half hours by car. There is no TGV serving the region, though you can pick this up from Rennes.

For further information on the region see www.normandy-tourism.org; www.bayeux-tourisme.com; www.calvados-tourisme.com. Books on Normandy include *Home & Dry in Normandy* by George East, published by Orion.

PICARDY
(departments of Aisne (02), Oise (60) and Somme (80))

This region was scarred by the battles of the trenches in the First World War. In recent years it has suffered from serious flooding, especially around Amiens, one of the region's most important centres. Oise, the department nearest to Paris, has over the last few years began to experience an influx of Parisians and some foreigners, many of the latter arriving at Beauvais airport on Ryanair flights from Glasgow, Dublin, Shannon and Stockholm. Beauvais is one hour from Paris, and only 12 miles from the stunning village of Gerberoy near the border with Normandy. Known as the City of Roses, Gerberoy has been designated one of France's 100 most beautiful villages. In Chantilly there is an English speaking association. Amiens is one and three quarter hours from Paris by train. 2005 saw the opening in Amiens of what is probably the largest cinema complex in France, save for that at Disneyland Paris.

PARIS AND THE ILE DE FRANCE
(departments of Ville de Paris (75), Hauts de Seine (92), Essonne (91), Seine et Marne (77), Seine-Saint-Denis (93), Val d'Oise (95), Val de Marne (94) and Yvelines (78))

France's capital city is divided into twenty *arrondissements*. Of the residential areas, the 3rd (part of the Latin quarter) and 4th, and to a lesser extent the 10th and 11th are quite youthful and lively, and the 5th, 6th (also part of the Latin quarter), 12th, 13th, 17th, 19th and 20th are most suited to families. Versailles and St. Germain on the outskirts of the capital are particularly popular with English speakers. As to property prices, the cheapest *arrondissements* are the 10th –15th, and 18th - 20th.

The cost of living in Paris is, not surprisingly, higher than elsewhere in France, but lower than in London. Much of the area around Paris remains unspoilt, though residential property within easy reach of the RER line serving the capital is expensive. The capital's tourist web site is www.paris-touristoffice.com. For information generally about Paris telephone 3975, from where you will be directed to the right government agency to deal with your enquiry.

There are many locations in Paris where English speakers can meet, and where you can obtain advice, assistance and a friendly welcome. A list is produced by the British Community Committee and can be obtained from the British Consulate. Britain, Ireland and Canada all have cultural centres in Paris, and there are several Anglican churches in and around Paris including St. Michael's Church in rue d'Aguesseau, and St. George's in Versailles, a couple of American churches and a Scottish Kirk. Several of these churches take considerable trouble to welcome newcomers, and have notice boards and newsletters where those seeking or offering accommodation or employment can place notices. St. Michael's periodically produces a booklet containing useful information for those arriving to live and work or study in Paris. There is a wide range of social and sports clubs and associations for English-speakers, offering a busy social life for those who wish to participate. Other useful sources of information include www.paris-anglo.com, www.americansinfrance.net, the English language newspapers, namely Fusac, France-USA Contacts and the Free Voice; the radio stations *Radio in English* and *Paris Live* Radio and their respective web sites www.radioinenglish.com and www.parislive.net. There are a number of English bookshops in Paris, including Shakespeare's, The Abbey Bookshop, The Village Voice and W.H. Smith.

There is a good selection of British, American and International schools in and around the capital, as well as English libraries, the American University of Paris, and many language schools where you can perfect your French, most notably *Alliance Française* which also offers courses about French civilisation, history and culture.

As to employment opportunities, apart from French newspapers and employment agencies, it is well-worth consulting the local Anglophone press, and the web sites of these publications and of the two English radio stations. You should also look at the web site of the British Chamber of Commerce in Paris, www.francobritishchambers.com. It lists job offers by member companies seeking bilingual staff, and includes contact details of over a dozen recruitment agencies and a facility for you to leave your CV. One agency that specialises in recruitment of bilingual secretaries, including for British law firms in the city, is Dorothy Danahy

(01.44.71.36.93; Recruitment@dorothy.fr).

You can fly direct to Paris Charles de Gaulle, or Paris Orly from around 20 airports in the UK (see Appendix 2 for details), with flights to Glasgow from Paris Beauvais.

CHAMPAGNE-ARDENNES
(departments of Ardennes (08), Aube (10), Marne (51), and Haute Marne (52))

The region is about two and a half hours' drive from Calais, with TGV links to the region's capital of Reims (pop. 200,000) and Troyes. It is famous for its champagne, and the fortified castles of the forests towards the Belgian border, and popular with tourists who come for the water sports on the region's lakes, hiking, horse riding and cycling. To date there have been relatively few settlers from the UK, despite the region's relative proximity to Paris and Brussels, its natural beauty and its low property prices. There are relatively few employment opportunities, though during the grape-picking season the wine industry employs an extra 45,000 people to assist in the harvest. The climate is fairly mild, though humid.

In Reims *L'Academie de Reims* has organised school boarding places (tel: 03 26 686000) and classes to assist children from age 8 upwards to integrate into the French education system.

For further information about the region see: www.ardennes.com; www.aube-champagne.com; www.tourisme-hautemarne.com; www.tourisme-champagne-ardenne.com

LORRAINE AND ALSACE
(departments of Moselle (57), Meuse (55), Meurthe et Moselle (54), Vosges (88), Bas Rhin (67) and Haut Rhin (68))

Whilst administratively separate, the two eastern regions of Lorraine (capital Metz) and Alsace (capital Strasbourg) are conveniently considered together. Both were at various times under German control, and Germanic influences are very apparent, with many of the population speaking German. These two regions are important agricultural and wine-growing areas, but also have heavily industrialised sectors with car manufacturing, electrical goods and paper-making taking primacy over the declining traditional industries of mining and steel manufacturing.

Metz is an elegant cosmopolitan city noted for its stunning public parks. The city of Nancy, also in Lorraine, is again an attractive city with many important buildings dating from the eighteenth century. Strasbourg is, of course, home to the European Parliament, but also to the Council of

Europe and the European Court. Both regions welcome large numbers of tourists each year, with some estimates putting the combined figure for both regions at over 15 million. Many of these visitors are on business trips, but large numbers come for the winter sports, the thermal resorts, the waterways and golf courses. The climate of these two regions is decidedly continental – hot in summer and very cold in winter. Property prices in Lorraine are well above the national average, and contrast markedly with Alsace where prices are still quite reasonable. Alsace is famous for its half-timbered houses.

There is a co-educational day school from nursery to *baccalauréat* in Strasbourg, the Lycée-Collège International des Pontonniers that has a British section (tel: 03 88 37 15 25). There is an Anglican church in Strasbourg and an English bookshop, the Bookworm (03 88 32 26 99). Useful web sites include: www.tourisme-mulhouse.com, www.crt-lorraine.fr

There are regular flights to London airports from Basel-Mulhouse, and Zurich and a flight from Strasbourg to London Gatwick (see Appendix 2 for further details). The journey time by car from Paris to Metz is three hours, from Paris to Strasbourg four and a half hours, and from Paris to Mulhouse is five hours. Train journey times are almost as long, though it is expected that the TGV line will open during 2006.

BRITTANY

(departments of Côte d'Armor (22), Finistere (29), Ille et Vilaines (35) and Morbihan (56))

Once one of the poorest regions of France, Brittany now has the lowest unemployment rate (8%) of all the regions of France. Today many residents are employed in tourism and industry (concentrated around Brest, Rennes and Lannion), as well as in the agricultural and fishing sectors. Brittany still has a very distinct Celtic identity with many historical and cultural links with Ireland, Wales and Cornwall. It is estimated that Breton is now the mother tongue of only just over a quarter of a million Bretons, over half of them in the most westerly department of Finistère. This is a fraction of the number who spoke the language a century ago, although interest in the language has grown in the last decade. Even though Breton is now taught in a number of schools in the region, and there are several radio stations that broadcast in Breton and newspapers that publish in the language, the language does not enjoy the protected status given to Welsh, for example. The region hosts regular festivals that see the arrival of other Celts from all over the world.

Brittany juts out into the sea and accordingly boasts a long coastline with many sandy beaches frequented by nearly four million holiday makers each year. The northern coast, which benefits from the Gulf Stream, is warmer than the south, and also rockier. There are significant English and Irish populations in Brittany, though much more spread out than those on the French Riviera, owing the to size of the region. They have been attracted by relatively low property prices, though the cost of property is now quite high in the coastal areas. Summers here are warm, and whilst winters are generally very rainy, they are mild.

Brittany has a number of facilities for English speakers. The best-served locality is certainly Rennes where the Franco-American Institute (tel: 02 99 79 20 57) has a lending library of English books, a weekly viewing of English films, and social and cultural activities. The city has a bilingual primary school (Ecole Jean Moulin, tel: 02 99 54 5704) and a *collège* and *lycée* with anglophone sections (tel: 0299544443). With increasing numbers of British families settling in different parts of the region, some local authorities have taken on specialist teachers to assist British and foreign children in the acquisition of French, and/or initiated French language courses aimed at English mother tongue speakers. There is an English bookshop at 4 rue de Vierges in Josselin in Morbihan. A number of French bookshops and newsagents stock a selection of English books (for details see www.brittany-angloinfo.com). The latter site also contains details of the dozen or so locations where you can see films in English, of the fifteen English and Irish pubs dotted around the region and of the various suppliers of English food and drink, as well as other items from the UK such as clothing. A recent additional source of information is the *Central Brittany Journal* that provides information about local businesses and services (see its web site at www.thecbj.com).

For further information on the region see the newspaper *Brittany News* and the web sites www.ukgrapevine.monsite.wanadoo.fr, www.annuaire-emeraude.com and www.tourismebretagne.com

As to air connections, Flybe now fly from Brest to Birmingham, Exeter, and Southampton and to Rennes from Southampton. Ryanair fly from Dinard to both London Luton and London Stansted. Air France and British Airways fly from Nantes Airport, just south of Brittany to London Gatwick. Aer Arann now fly to Lorient from London Luton There are a number of flights to Paris, including from Lorient airport. There are many regular ferry crossings to the UK ports of Poole, Weymouth, Portsmouth, Plymouth and Bournemouth. The journey from Rennes to Paris by TGV is only two hours, compared to three and a half by road.

WESTERN LOIRE
(departments of Loire Atlantique (44), Maine et Loire (49), Mayenne (53), Sarthe (72) and Vendée (85))

This is a quiet, peaceful region. Towards the Atlantic coast the terrain is flat and wooded, whereas in the east the land consists largely of cultivated fields. It is an important agricultural region, with mild winters and hot summers. Other industries include fishing, shipbuilding, car manufacturing at the immense Renault factory in Le Mans, and of course tourism which is concentrated along the 100 miles or so of Atlantic coastline, with the long wide beaches at La Baule being particularly worth a visit. The region's administrative capital is Nantes, with a population of nearly half a million. Property prices in this region have been low, but are not surprisingly higher in the coastal areas. La Vendée is increasingly popular with the British thanks to its excellent climate, and the cost of buying property there has risen significantly in recent years.

There are relatively few facilities for English speakers, though for those living in the northern part of the region, the city of Rennes is easily accessible. The city has a Franco-American cultural centre, and primary and secondary schools catering for English-speakers (for further information see above under Brittany). There is a private Catholic boarding school for English speakers at Chavagnes (www.chavagnes.org, tel: 02 51 42 39 82).

Flybe flies from Southampton to La Rochelle and Rennes, and from Birmingham to La Rochelle, and Ryanair flies from London Stansted to La Rochelle. There are also flights from Nantes International Airport to London Gatwick operated by Air France and British Airways. Nantes is two hours from Paris by the TGV, though by car the journey time is nearly twice that.

For further information on this region see www.ukgrapevine.monsite.wanadoo.fr, www.vendee-tourisme.com and for the Loire generally see www.westernloire.com

THE LOIRE VALLEY

(departments of Cher (18), Eure et Loire (28), Indre (36), Indre et Loire (37), Loir et Cher (41) and Loiret (45))

Sharing its name with France's longest river, the region is almost entirely flat, extremely fertile and noted in particular for its wine growing areas and its many *châteaux* dating from the sixteenth century. The prosperous cities of Chartres, Tours and Orléans have all seen substantial growth over the last decade. The latter is a former capital of France and was of particular importance during the Hundred Years War. Whilst the region is extremely popular with British tourists, who tend to visit a *château* or two and sample wine on a brief stop over on their way further south, until recently very few British chose to settle here. Accordingly there is little in the way of anglophone social, cultural and support groups and activities. There is a bookshop in Tours where you can purchase books in English (*La Boîte à Livres de l'Etranger*, 02 47 05 67 29). As the region is particularly flat, it is easy to explore by cycle, especially now that there is a traffic free cycle trail from Angers to Tours.

Ryanair flies daily from Stansted to Tours. There is a bus service from the airport into town. Parking at the airport is currently free. There is an excellent train service from St Malo to Nantes, and the train journey from London to Tours via Lille takes four and a half hours. Chartres is less than an hour from Paris by train. For further information on the region see www.loirevalleytourisme.com (tel. 02 38799528)

BURGUNDY AND FRANCH COMTE

(departments of Côte-d'Or (21), Nievre (58), Saône et Loire (71) and Yonne (89) and Doubs (25), Jura (39), Haute-Saône (70) and the Territoire de Belfort (90)).

Burgundy is steeped in history, with the Burgundians having fought on the English side during the Hundred Years war, and having handed Joan of Arc over to the English after capturing her. Accordingly Joan of Arc does not feature greatly in the Burgundians' concept of their French identity, which perhaps explains why many Britons find them particularly friendly. Burgundy is almost entirely agricultural and rural with very little industry at all. The region is famous for its culinary arts, and of course its wines, though tourists are also attracted by the extensive network of navigable canals and rivers, its lakes ideal for water sports and its cultural and historic past. There are few golf courses here. The region's administrative centre is Dijon.

The Burgundians have yet to see a large influx of foreigners, although in some areas Parisians purchasing second homes have caused property prices to rise. The climate here is hot in the summer and generally cold during the winter months. Those settling near the river Saône should note that areas around the river between Lyon and Mâcon have been flooded on a number of occasions over the last few years. The region is beginning to see the arrival of some Britons, which explains the recent opening of a British food stall at Villefranche-sur- Saône (www.paulshop.com, tel 04 74 05 93 49). The Swedish company Ikea has recently opened a large store in Dijon.

For further information about Dijon see www.dijon-tourisme.com and about Auxerre www.auxerre.com

To the east, Franche-Comté is largely mountainous, or populated with thick pine forests and rich wildlife. Its landscape resembles that of its Swiss neighbour. This region does not see many foreign tourists, and very few British chose to settle here, despite the low property prices.

As to flights, there are no airports in Burgundy with flights to the UK. There is, however, a wide range of UK destinations with direct flights from

Basel-Mulhouse and Geneva (just over the Swiss border). For further details see Appendix 2. The journey time by TGV from Dijon to Paris is one hour forty minutes, and from Besançon to Paris two hours 40 minutes. By road, Dijon is a three-hour drive from Paris.

POITOU-CHARENTES
(departments of Charente (16), Charente-Maritime (17), Deux-Sèvres (79) and Vienne (86))

This region is bordered by the river Loire to the north, and the Gironde to the south, and lies between the Atlantic Coast and the Massif Central. In recent years it has become particularly popular with the British attracted by the sunny climate, the sandy beaches, and the peace and calm of the region. La Rochelle, a Protestant stronghold during the years of religious strife in France, is particularly interesting historically, and in recent years has become well-known for the environmental friendly policies adopted by the local council: to travel around the town you will have to hire a bicycle, or one of the electric cars that are available, or walk on foot. For further information see www.larochelle-tourisme.com

The Ile de Ré and the Ile d'Oleron are both stunning, and would be delightful places to live. The most important town in the region is Poitiers, famous for its Futuroscope. This popular attraction has its own train station, distinct from Poitiers Ville (for details see www.futuroscope.com).

Employment opportunities in the region are somewhat limited – most of the region is rural. On the coast there is a demand in the tourist sector, and at Poitiers *Le Futuroscope* is an important employer. Poitiers has also experienced growth in the information technology sector.

There are now several shops in the region that sell British food items, others that sell books in English and quite a few English and Irish pubs. The Anglican church is also well represented in the region. Details can be obtained from the new Poitou-Charentes web site operated by www.angloinfo.com, and also from www.frenchnews.com. Information on Charente-Martime can be obtained from the web site of the department's tourist board: www.charente-maritime.org. Recently a number of public libraries have started to stock English books, including that at Gourville in Charente.

You can fly direct from La Rochelle to London Stansted with Ryanair, and to Birmingham and Southampton with Flybe. There is a bus service from the airport at La Rochelle into town. From Poitiers there is a Ryanair service to Stansted, but currently no bus from the airport to the town. Parking is free. Just to the north of the region British Airways and Air France operate a service from Nantes to London Gatwick. Poitiers, Angoulême, La Rochelle and Niort are all linked to Paris via the TGV.

LIMOUSIN AND AUVERGNE

(departments of Corrèze (19), Creuse ((23), and Haute-Vienne (87))
and (Allier (03), Cantal (15), Haute-Loire (43),
and Puy-de-Dôme (63))

These are two of the most remote, unspoiled and sparsely populated regions of France. If you are in search of employment there are few opportunities. On the other hand, if you can work from home, are in search of a very quiet life, and do not mind the cold winters (especially in the Auvergne), then you may find these regions ideal. Certainly property prices are much lower than elsewhere in France. Limousin has some 3,000 lakes, and is almost totally unspoilt. With an ageing and shrinking population as its younger inhabitants leave in search of work in Paris and other large cities, there is an ample supply of property, much of it suitable for development as a *chambre d'hôte*. The Auvergne boasts dramatic geography, a legacy to its volcanic past (and indeed present), including its thermal springs.

The British interest in the Auvergne has not surprisingly fallen off dramatically since the airport at Clermont-Ferrand (Aulnat) lost the Ryanair flights. The numbers of tourist visitors to the region have been down for both 2004 and 2005. In truth the region has not adapted to the demands of modern day tourists, with all shops closing on Mondays, even at the height of the holiday season. It is impossible to lunch or dine late.

The local authorities in Limousin remain convinced that they can attract Britons to the area. Indeed, a new terminal building has just been opened at Limoges, with Ryanair flying to Stansted, and Flybe to Southampton. The airport will open up the region including the Creuse, Indre, parts of Poitou-Charentes, Corrèze and the Dordogne. At present there is no bus service from the airport into Limoges, but parking is still free. There are also plans to develop the airport at Brive. For those living in the northwest of the region, there is a flight to London Stansted from Poitiers.

There was substantial interest shown in Limousin at the French Property Exhibition at Olympia in the autumn 2005. Those contemplating a move to the area, especially Creuse, should take a look at www.centralfranceinfoguide.com, run by Sheena Pacetti, a friendly Scottish lady who has lived in the area for several years. Central France Information Guide can also be contacted on 05 55807361.

There are relatively few services for British expatriates, although in Corrèze in Limousin there are British grocery stores in Brive (tel: 05 55 25 09 54), and in Beaulieu-sur-Dordogne (tel: 05 55 28 69 34). In Creuse, also in Limousin, some branches of Leclerc and Intermarché have recently started stocking a range of British food products.

For further information on Limousin see the web site of the region's tourist board www.tourismelimousin.com and also www.tourisme-hautevienne.com, www.tourisme-creuse.com and www.cg19.fr.

Limoges is three hours from Paris by train, and Clermont-Ferrand four hours. There is a TGV service planned that will connect Limoges and Brive with Paris and Toulouse. Whilst the airport at Clermont-Ferrand has no direct flights to the UK, there are flights to most French cities and a number of European cities.

RHÔNE-ALPES
(departments of Ain (01), Ardèche (07), Drôme (26), Isère (38), Loire (42), Rhône (69), Savoie (73) and Haute-Savoie (74))

The Rhône-Alpes is bordered by Italy to the east and the Massif Central to the west. Lyon, the region's capital and France's gastronomic capital, dates back to Roman times, when it was known as Lugdunum. It boasts many historical sites, several of which form part of a site classified by UNESCO as a world heritage site. A considerable number of these are illuminated after nightfall. Lyon has an efficient network of trams and buses, as well as a metro. A pass is available from the tourist office that gives you access to all the main museums and public transport at a cost of €18 for one day, with reduced daily rates for two and three day passes. In an attempt to reduce congestion the local council has provided 1,000 bicycles available to hire from the city's railway stations. The first half-hour is free, with a modest hourly rate thereafter. The tourist office publishes a bilingual French/English newsletter listing local events and containing practical information. The city has a population of just over a million, with the region's second city Grenoble having around 400,000 inhabitants. Both cities have increased dramatically in size in the last twenty-five years, and many jobs have been created in and around Lyon, and in the area between Grenoble and Geneva. The same is true of St. Etienne.

The region is characterised by very hot summers and very cold winters. There is a wide range of leisure pursuits, including white-water rafting, canoeing and hiking, as well as skiing.

There are significant numbers of Britons living and working in and around Lyon, Grenoble and St. Etienne, and also in Annecy and Evian. In Lyon there is an active *Association France-Grande-Bretagne* (tel: 04 78 28 41 81). You can also obtain information relating to the region, and the various British clubs, associations and help-group by contacting the British Consulate in Lyon (tel: 04 72 77 81 70), or accessing the consulate's web site via www.amb-grandebretagne.fr (click on "English"). In Grenoble there is a library stocking books in English (04 76 42 43 91), and a cultural association, the Open House Association (04 76 52 44 30), which runs a range of activities and is well worth contacting.

Owing to the large numbers of English speakers working in the region there are now several options for educating your children, including state-run international schools. In Lyon there is the *Cité-Scolaire Internationale de Lyon* (tel: 04 78 69 60 06), and also two private international schools, the *Lycée Multilingue de Lyon* (04 78 23 22 63), and the recently opened *International School of Lyon* (04 26 68 70 08). In Grenoble, the *Cité-Scolaire Internationale Stendhal* (04 76 54 83 83), is a co-educational state international school. Towards Geneva there is also a private co-educational school – the *Lycée Collège International Ferney-Voltaire*, in which part of the curriculum is based on the UK national curriculum.

There are bookshops in both Lyon and Grenoble that stock English-language books, in particular Discovery in Lyon (tel: 04 78 62 76 58) where you will also find a selection of British foods and drinks. Practical guides to living in Lyon and Grenoble are available from the Association France-Grande-Bretagne (tel: 04 78 28 41 81). For Lyon it is also worth looking at the web site www.families-on-the-move.com. Ikea have recently opened a large store in St. Etienne.

Air France flies to Lyon from Heathrow, British Airways flies to Lyon from Heathrow, Birmingham and Manchester, easyJet from Stansted and Thomsonfly from Coventry, Doncaster-Sheffield and Bournemouth. To the east there are many flights to UK destinations from Geneva (i.e. all London airports, Belfast, Bristol, Edinburgh, Glasgow, Leeds/Bradford, Liverpool, Manchester, Newcastle, Nottingham and Southampton (see Appendix 2). Ryanair fly to Grenoble and St. Etienne from London Stansted. The A6 motorway, and a TGV line run between Lyon and Paris. By train the journey to Lyon is two hours, with a journey by car taking over twice as long. Grenoble is three hours by train from Paris.

The web site for the Lyon tourist office is www.lyon-france.com, and that for the region Rhône-Alpes is www.rhonealpes-tourisme.com (and also www.rhonealpes-mountains.com). Information can also be obtained from www.eviantourisme.com

AQUITAINE
(departments of Dordogne (24), Gironde (33), Landes (40), Lot- et-Garonne (47) and Pyrénées-Atlantiques (64))

This diverse region includes the valleys of the Dordogne, the Basque country, the chic resort of Biarritz and the Pyrenees. The capital of the region is Bordeaux, a thriving prosperous city with a population of nearly three quarters of a million people. Other main towns include Bergerac, Pau, Périgueux and Sarlat. This is an important agricultural region, with tourism forming a major economic rôle in coastal areas. The summers here are hot and dry, and the winters warm and mild. During the Middle Ages Aquitaine was ruled by the English monarchy, and for more than two decades now the British have been settling in the area, notably the Dordogne and Lot-et-Garonne, where property prices are quite high.

Employment prospects are greatest in Bordeaux and in the tourist coastal towns. There is a wide range of sporting activities, especially water sports with surfing being extremely popular owing to the excellent conditions.

Options for educating your children include the Bordeaux International School (05 57 87 02 11, www.bordeaux-intl-school.com) which in part follows the UK national curriculum, but also has several French nationals on its staff. There is also the Collège (Cheverus) and the Lycée (François Magendie) each of which have international sections (tel: 05 57 57 1952). There are a number of other facilities for English-speakers in Bordeaux including the bookshop Bradley's (05 56 52 10 57), a cinema showing films in English, Barclays Bank, a branch of Bodyshop and a shop selling British food items, The Tea Cosy. Elsewhere in the region there is a Best of British grocery store in Périgueux, *Le Magasin Anglais* (tel: 06 33 92 22 56) in Eymet, and a Barclays in Biarritz.

There are many different expatriate sporting and social groups, and details can be obtained from the Bordeaux British Community Association (www.bordeauxbritish.com). Information on the many British businesses can be found on the web site of *French News* www.french-news.com and is available also from the British Consulate in Bordeaux (see Appendix 1 for contact details). *French News* now publishes a regular supplement entitled Aquitaine News.

You can fly direct to Bordeaux from London Gatwick, Bristol, Southampton and Dublin. There are also direct flights from Stansted to Biarritz, Bergerac and Pau, and from Birmingham, Bristol and Southampton to Bergerac. Ryanair has a flight from Dublin to Biarritz. The area can also be reached from Plymouth via Santander in northern Spain with Brittany ferries.

The journey time by train from Paris to Bordeaux is 3 hours (nearly twice this by car), and from Paris to Pau is 8 hours.

For further information about Aquitaine see www.bordeaux-city.com; www.paysdedordogne-tourisme.com

MIDI-PYRÉNÉES

(departments of Ariège (09), Aveyron (12), Haute-Garonne (31), Gers
(32), Lot (46), Hautes-Pyrénées (65), Tarn (81), and Tarn-et-Garonne
(82))

The largest region of France, the mid-Pyrenees is home to the rivers
Lot, Aveyron, Tarn and Garonne. All the departments apart from Haute-
Garonne are very sparsely populated. By far the largest population centre
is Toulouse, the region's capital, which has a population of over 600,000.
The city is the birthplace of Concorde and is home to the French (and
much of the European) aerospace industry and to the headquarters of
Airbus. It has a thriving high-tech sector. A number of foreign companies
have a presence here, including Lucas Aerospace. Apart from in Toulouse
itself, most employment opportunities are in the agricultural and tourism
sectors, in the latter case in an around Lourdes which welcomes several
million tourists per year, and in the ski resorts and thermal baths of the
Pyrenees.

In most of the region house prices are low. They are highest in and
around Toulouse, and also in Lot where a large number of properties have
been purchased as second homes. As to educational options, the Lycée
International Victor Hugo in Colomiers is a French state school with a
British section covering all school ages (see its web site
http://pedagogie.ac-toulouse.fr/lyc-international-colomiers/ - go to *Le Pôle
International* and scroll to the bottom of the list to find *La Section
Britannique* or telephone the school on 05 61 15 9494). The private
International School of Toulouse is also located in Colomiers (see its web
site at www.intst.net or tel: 05.62.74.26.74). You will find English
bookshops in Toulouse (including *La Librairie Anglaise*) and also in
Montcuq in the Lot, and an Anglo-American library in Toulouse, as well as
an English language library at Toulouse university. British foodstuffs, and
other items from the UK, can be purchased at Simply British in Foix, one
hour's drive south of Toulouse (e-mail simplybritfoix@aol,.com, tel: 05 61
50 40 92), and at *La Boutique Anglaise* in Naucelle (tel: 05 65 72 45 68).
A new web site for the Anglophone community in the region that is well
worth visiting is www.pyreneespeople.com. There is a branch of Virgin
Megastore in the city.

There are many other businesses run by British and Irish ex-patriots in
the region as well as a wide range of sports and social clubs and
associations. Details of these, and of the eight or nine Anglican churches
in the region can be obtained from the British consulate in Bordeaux.
Those contemplating setting up a business in the area should make
contact with the British International Business Network Toulouse
(BIBNT), a non-profit making association that offers advice and arranges

seminars. Contact Lynda Racher on 06 89360417 and see their web site www.bibnt.com.

There are flights to Toulouse from London Gatwick, London Stansted, Aberdeen, Birmingham, Bristol, Edinburgh, Glasgow, Manchester and Southampton. Ryanair flies to Rodez from Stansted. By rail, Toulouse is a little over five hours from Paris, with a route also to Lille from where you can catch the Motorail all the way to Toulouse. You should allow a good seven hours for the motorway link from Paris to Toulouse.

For information about Toulouse see www.ot-toulouse.fr, and for the region generally www.tourisme-midi-pyrenees.org. The web site of the tourist board for the department of Aveyron is www.aveyron.com

LANGUEDOC-ROUSSILLON
(departments of Aude (11), Gard (30), Hérault (34), Lozère (48) and Pyrénées-Orientales (66))

This region, which stretches from the Spanish border along the Mediterranean coast to the Camargue and onwards towards the French Riviera, has wonderful sandy beaches, and numerous interesting seaside ports, such as those of Collioure and Céret. Water sports are extremely popular, as are horse riding and walking in the Massif Central to the north, and the Pyrenees to the south. The towns of Carcassonne and Nîmes are reminders of the region's Roman past. Bullfighting is still popular, especially in Nîmes. The region's capital Montpellier has a thriving high tech sector. Other important centres include Perpignan, Béziers, Alès and Narbonne. All of the departments, with the exception of Pyrénées-Orientales, have suffered significant flood damage over recent years. Nîmes has been particularly severely hit, including in September 2005. The cost of property is generally far lower than on the Côte d'Azur to the east, though in the coastal ports prices are high.

This is an agricultural region, with much of the land being devoted to vineyards. Not surprisingly, the tourist industry also plays a major part in the local economy, with the number of visitors now approaching 15 million per year. The climate on the coast is very hot and dry during the summer months, and mild in the winter. Inland, winters can be rather cold. Besides the coastal resorts, tourists are attracted by historic abbeys, the fortified cathedral at Béziers, and the site of the oldest human remains in France, at Tautevel, not far from Perpignan. Most of the region's inhabitants live near the coast. Like the Alpes-Maritimes to the east, Languedoc-Roussillon has seen a large influx of people from other parts of France, and indeed from other European countries.

May and June 2005 saw outbreaks of racial violence between local Algerians and gypsy families living in Perpignan. At one stage 1,000

Algerians protested in the streets after one of their number was lynched. 160 gypsy families took refuge in Montpellier to avoid the violence. At one point there were 1,000 police and soldiers patrolling the streets of Perpignan, and Nicolas Sarkozy visited the town to call for calm and to throw his weight behind the forces of law and order.

There are a number of expatriate associations and groups, including the British Cultural Association, the Franco-Scottish Association, Brits Around Béziers (04 68 83 38 54) and www.britsnimes.com (04 66 26 07 34). In addition to the Anglican churches, there is an international Methodist church in Narbonne (www.methodist-narbonne.org; 04 68 76 58 54). A new cricket club is starting in Hérault (contact Peter Sandison on 04 67 28 52 03).

As to schooling, the Ecole Privée Bilingue Internationale, just outside Montpellier, caters for children from nursery school to sixth form (04 67 70 78 44). There is now an English lending library in Arlès-sur-Tech. Montpellier boasts three English bookshops (The Bookshop, 04 67 66 09 08; As You Like It, 04 67 66 22 90) and *La Maison de Cambridge*. British foodstuffs and other items are available from a branch of the Best of British grocery chain, and also from *Au goût anglais*. The Swedish giant Ikea has recently opened a large store in Montpellier.

Ryanair flies to Montpellier from Stansted, and British Airways/GB Airways flies to Montpellier from Gatwick. Nîmes airport (with Ryanair links to Stansted, Luton and Liverpool) has recently escaped the threat of closure. Perpignan is served by BMI services from Southampton and Birmingham, and Ryanair from Stansted. Lastly, Ryanair also flies to Carcassonne from Stansted. There is a TGV service from Paris to Montpellier (4 and a half hours), and there are also TGV services to Béziers, Perpignan and Narbonne. There is a direct Eurostar link from Lille to Montpellier and a Motorail link to Narbonne from Calais.

Useful web sites include: www.ville-perigueux.fr

PROVENCE
(departments of Alpes de Haute-Provence (04), Hautes-Alpes (05), Bouches-du-Rhône (13), Var (83), Vaucluse (84) and Alpes-Maritimes (06))

This region occupies the area between the Rhône to the west and the Italian border to the east, and stretches from the Mediterranean in the south, to the Alps in the north. It includes the fashionable Riviera playgrounds of the rich and famous, as well as remote mountain areas. The regional capital Marseille, with a population of about 1 million, was for many years the undisputed second largest city in France, though now competes with Lyon for this title. The city is also one of France's major ports with much maritime traffic to north Africa, but also to north America and other destinations across the globe. Other important towns include Toulon (with a population of around 400,000), Nice (pop. around 350,000), Aix-en-Provence, Arles, Avignon and Cannes.

Parts of Vaucluse and Bouches-du-Rhône suffered from serious flooding in 2002 and 2003, and further east the summer of 2003 saw over 20,000 hectares of woodland destroyed by fires in the Var. The Alpes-Maritimes is situated in an earthquake zone and saw a substantial loss of life and considerable destruction in the last earthquake in 1887. The region is also subject to much more frequent earth tremors. New safety building regulations were introduced in 1994, primarily covering apartment blocks, though the extent of compliance with these is questionable. Property prices in Provence vary considerably, with property being cheap inland, but much more expensive along the coast, especially around Marseille, Toulon and Nice, and in and around the fashionable resorts such as St. Tropez and Cannes. The likelihood of a further earthquake in the Alpes-Maritimes at some point during the next 200 years does not appear to restrict the rise in property prices in the department. Even these prices compare favourably with the cost of property in Monaco.

In some parts of Provence, especially in Alpes-Maritimes, property owners are able to let out their properties during much of the summer, from as early as May to as late as mid-October, charging far more than they could per month on a standard rental. Indeed, some owner-occupiers let out their own homes for a month or even longer, and take their holidays elsewhere, move in with friends or find cheap short-term accommodation.

Tourism is a major industry in much of Provence, including green tourism, and hunting. Visitors are also attracted by the historical sites, such as the Roman remains at Arles and Orange, and the former papal palace at Avignon.

It is worthwhile asking to go onto the Marseille British consulate's e-mailing list (contact Pascale.Gauthier-Keogh@fco.gov.uk). You will receive details of a host of social and other events throughout Provence.

There is a sizeable English speaking population in Marseille, and information on English speaking businesses, and social events can be obtained from the British consulate in Marseille. There is an Anglican church in Marseille and also branches of the Association France-Grande-Bretagne and of the Royal British Legion. Books in English are available at Ad hoc Books (04 91 33 51 92). British food can be purchased in the various branches of *Torrefaction Noailles* around the city. British shops in the city include the Bodyshop, the Virgin Megastore and Burberrys.

Aix-en-Provence is a particularly attractive city that does not suffer a great deal from the side effects of tourism. The Anglo-American Group of Provence (04 42 24 03 40) offers a considerable range of social activities, and practical assistance for those moving to Aix. It also operates a sizeable English language library, for which a modest subscription is payable. The town has a branch of the Best of British grocery store (04 42 26 47 99), an adjacent bookshop that sells English books and a branch of the Bodyshop. There are several educational options, including the Ecole Val Saint André, the Lycée International Général et Technologique Luynes, the British American Institute and the International Bilingual School of Provence. In addition there is a Protestant school for nursery children up to 18, providing a French-based education.

In the Var a useful source of information is the web site of Var Village Voice, the local English language newspaper (www.varvillagevoice.com; 0494 04 49 60). English language bookshops include the Castle Bookshop in Fayence (04 94 84 04 16), and Heidi's Bookshop in Villecroze, Draguignan. In Toulon you will find a branch of the Association France-Grande-Bretagne, and an Anglican church in St. Tropez. In Vaucluse there is an English library in Malaucène, the Beaumont Library (04 90 65 25 60).

There are English and Irish pubs scattered at various locations in Provence, mainly near the coast and in the larger cities, with a much higher concentration eastwards from St. Tropez to the Italian border. Those not far from the A8 motorway in the Var or Alpes-Maritimes who enjoy a traditional fish and chip supper should pay a visit to Jim Cookson at *Les Arbousiers* restaurant, situated on the shores of Lac St Cassien a short drive from Exit 39. You can swim in this large lake or hire a pedal boat. Another English run establishment, worth a visit for a traditional Sunday lunch, is *Le Relais des Coches* in Tourrettes-sur-Loup (04 93 24 30 24).

Historically the Alpes-Maritimes has been the most popular French destination for British expatriates, both as a holiday location, and as a place to live, with the Victorians playing a major rôle in the development of the area, including the construction of the larger hotels along *Le Promenade des Anglais* in Nice. This remains true today and explains why there is a whole host of different services aimed at English speaking communities, ranging from several international schools, to churches, to English and Irish pubs, to grocery stores. This small corner of France certainly has the most favoured climate in the country, with winters being extremely mild.

Whilst the unemployment rate in the Alpes-Maritimes is certainly higher than the UK, there are numerous English speakers and other foreigners working here. The region boasts the largest business park in Europe at Sophia Antipolis where several large British and other international companies have offices. Sophia Antipolis is blighted with traffic congestion in the morning and evenings, has inadequate road signs and has only very poor public transport facilities. Despite this, property prices rental levels in Sophia are high. There are large numbers of immigrants working in hotels and restaurants in the department, mostly Portuguese, Italians, Spaniards and Algerians. Nevertheless, there is still a substantial shortage of labour for this type of work during the summer, in large part due to low salary levels and the high cost of accommodation on the Riviera.

Apart from perhaps the French capital, the Alpes-Maritimes has a higher concentration of English speakers than any other area in France. There are accordingly more facilities for the Anglophone communities than elsewhere, with many British people being employed in the businesses that provide them. There are several schools catering for foreigners. Mougins School (www.mougins-school.com, 04 93 21 04 00) is a private school with a British-based curriculum with primarily British teaching staff, though only around a third of the pupils are British. The International School of Nice (www.isn-nice.org, 04 93 21 04 00) is also private. It also has an English head, and a considerable number of British staff, though it has more of an American and European feel about it and students take the international baccalaureate. The Centre International de Valbonne (www.civissa.org, 04 92 96 52 54) is a French state secondary school with an Anglophone section, costing around 1,500 euros per year. The International School of Monaco is the newest private international school, with a total fees package higher than both Mougins and the International School of Nice. For a full list of international and private schools claiming to offer a bilingual education see www.angloinfo.com

There are English language libraries in Nice (The English American Library, 04 93 16 96 49), Monaco (the Princess Grace Irish Library) and Vence, and also several English bookshops in the region, namely Antibes Books, the Cannes English Bookshop, The Cat's Whiskers in Nice, Scruples in Monaco and the English Book Centre in Valbonne (see www.angloinfo.com for full contact details). There are a number of outlets selling British food and other products, including Geoffrey's in Antibes (04 92 90 66 40) and Brittain's Home Store in Valbonne (04 93 42 01 70). Some of the French supermarkets have a small selection of British items, including Champion in Mougins and Antibes, Carrefour in Antibes and Galeries Lafayette in Cap 3000 at St. Laurent du Var. As to the large British chains, Virgin Megastore has a branch in Nice, and the Bodyshop has branches in Nice Etoile and Cap 3000. British banks represented in the area include Barclays, with a number of branches in the area and currently a large billboard to welcome arrivals at Nice airport. The Abbey National, which had several branches in the area, has been taken over by BNP ParisBas.

As to doctors and dentists, many of those practising in the Alpes-Maritimes claim to speak English, although few do so well. There is a British General Practitioner not far from Mougins, Dr. Ireland (04 93 12 95 66). British dentists include Helen Giacommi in Cagnes-sur-Mer (04 93 22 92 77) and Robert Hempleman in Cannes (04 93 38 10 83). The French orthodontist Dr. Dossou in rue d'Antibes in Cannes underwent orthodontic training in both France and the United States. There will shortly be a retirement home catering primarily for the expatriate community. The Sunny Bank retirement home is due to open in Mouans Sartoux in the summer of 2006 (contact Peter Durlacher on 04 93 900216).

There are several English language magazines and newspapers. New publications appear from time to time, though in many cases go out of business after only a few months or years. The longest established is the *Riviera Reporter* that also has an extremely useful web site www.rivierareporter.com. Other established publications include the *Riviera Times*. The most popular English language radio station is *Riviera Radio* whose website is also well worth a visit, www.rivieraradio.mc. Other stations broadcasting to the area include *The Breeze*, and *Radio International*.

There are numerous clubs and associations in the Alpes-Maritimes run for and by English-speaking expatriates, including the British Association (with several branches in the area including in Nice, Cannes, Menton, and Monaco), the Auld Alliance, the Commonwealth Club and the *Association France-Grande-Bretagne*. There are a host of other different interest clubs ranging from amateur dramatics, to rugby and cricket, to the Oxbridge Set, to party political groups. There are also several Anglican churches in the area, a non-Anglican Christian Fellowship group that meets in Sophia Antipolis and non-conformist international churches in Cannes and Nice (for full details consult www.angloinfo.com or www.rivierareporter.com or telephone the British Consulate in Marseille or the Vice-consulate in Nice - see Appendix 1 for contact details). A very useful source of information and advice is Adapt in France (04 93 65 33 79) based in Sophia Antipolis. There are different rates of membership fees payable, depending on your requirements. It is well-used by English speakers, and has a library of resources, and runs over a dozen different workshops on topics such as working in France, setting up a business, schooling etc. Information can be obtained by consulting www.adaptinfrance.org. A particularly helpful website, packed with information in English, is www.amb-Côtedazur.com. Wheelchair users in the region can contact S. Odgers, odger1@yahoo.com for information about facilities in the region.

As to job opportunities, many of those British who go to the Côte d'Azur to work, or in search of work, find employment in businesses that primarily serve the English speaking or international communities living there, such as many of the teachers in the international schools, employees of estate agencies, letting agencies and banks, those working in the yachting industry, domestic staff, security guards, chauffeurs, gardeners, and property maintenance staff. A considerable number start their own business, ranging from hairdressing to offering insurance and financial advice to expatriates. An invaluable source of information for those in business, or those contemplating going into business is the local British Chamber of Commerce (see its web site www.bccriviera.org).

French employers seem a little wary of taking on British staff, and if you do not speak much French your prospects are not good. There are, however, some British who manage to obtain positions with French employers, and some who succeed in gaining promotion. They generally have a good knowledge of written and spoken French, and a willingness to adapt. In the summer months there is a major shortage of labour, and for those in search of a temporary job in a hotel, or in a restaurant, the prospects are good. The pay is low, however, and accommodation costs in the region are high. For further information see the web sites www.anpe.fr and www.crij.org/nice. These two organisations have jointly produced the *Guide des jobs d'été*. It is published annually and should be obtainable by telephoning any office of the ANPE in the Alpes-Maritimes (such as one of the Nice offices, 04 93 97 90 00), or the CRIJ Côte d'Azur on 04 93 80 93 93.

There are flights to Nice from all of London's main four airports, as well as from Belfast, Bristol, Edinburgh, Glasgow, Leeds/Bradford, Liverpool, Manchester, Newcastle, Nottingham East Midlands and Dublin. Although Nice is only France's tenth largest city, it has the country's second busiest airport, with many reasonably priced flights to Paris and other European cities. Airport Transfer Services provide a door-to-door minibus service to Nice airport. Taxi operators include *Taxi David* who advertises a day and night airport transfer service covering Monaco, Nice and Cannes (0609525425).

There are flights to Marseille from London Gatwick, and Dublin, and to Toulon from London Stansted.

By train (TGV) Marseille is now only four hours from Paris and seven hours from London Waterloo. Nice is around nine and a half hours from London by train. Eurostar and Motorail have services as far as Avignon. The motorway journey from Paris to Marseille takes around seven hours, and from Paris to Nice takes a little over eight hours.

CORSICA

The *Ile de Béauté*, as the island is affectionately termed by the French, is 160 km from the Côte d'Azur, though only half that distance from the Italian coastline. The weather is hot during the summer, and mild but also windy during the winter months. The island has two departments, Corse du Sud (20A) and Haute-Corse (20B), with a total population of around 250,000. The capital is Ajaccio, though the largest town on the island is Bastia. The island remains unspoilt, thanks in large part to its small population, and to the restrictions on building and developing imposed by the local authorities. The island has a generous supply of sandy beaches, although much of the coast is rocky. There are many opportunities for sport enthusiasts, especially water sports, but also rock-climbing and even skiing.

There is little industry here, with the island being known for its agricultural products, especially wine and citrus fruits. There are very limited job opportunities apart from in the agricultural and tourist sectors. There are few English speakers here, and no international school. Children are often obliged to learn the Corsican language. There is a small university, though the range of courses is quite restricted.

Property prices are high on the island, to a large extent because of the shortage of properties and the restrictions imposed by local government. Those who decide to buy here frequently encounter problems in the conveyancing transaction, owing to the fact that property is often in the names of several people, all of whose consents are required for the sale to proceed. You may find that it takes a considerable time to complete the purchase.

GB Airways fly from London Gatwick to Bastia. Otherwise there are flights to the island from Paris and Nice. For ferry crossings to Corsica from Marseille, Toulon and Nice contact SNCM 02074914968 web site: southernferries@seafrance.fr. The crossing time varies between five and ten hours depending upon the service used. There are also (shorter) ferry crossings from the Italian ports of Savone and Livourne. For information about Corsica it is well worth taking a look at www.visit-corsica.com and www.tourismecorse.com

Chapter Two

FINDING ACCOMMODATION

Renting a property in France

If you envisage only a temporary stay in France, or are uncertain how long you will be there, it is advisable to rent rather than purchase. Indeed renting initially has distinct advantages even for those intending a permanent move. Whilst property prices remain significantly lower than in the UK, apart from in Paris and the Riviera, there are significantly higher costs involved in both buying and selling a property in France than in the UK. Renting a property gives you the time needed to familiarise yourself with an area and its amenities, and to ensure that it does indeed suit you and your family before making a significant investment that could prove an expensive mistake.

Advantages of renting include being able to put off the high initial costs of purchasing a home, and a long-term commitment to monthly mortgage repayments. You may also find that you can rent a larger property than you could afford to buy – depending on the age of your children, you may feel it makes more sense to buy a small property for the future and rent it out for the moment. Finding and deciding upon a property to rent generally requires much less time and effort. It can provide an excellent flexible short or medium term solution to your housing needs. In addition, some people prefer to retain their property in the UK and rent it out, whilst themselves renting in France, given the rate of increase in property prices in the UK over the past decade.

The drawbacks of putting off a purchase include the present rate of increase in property prices in most areas, which could mean that you are priced out of the market, and the fact that those over 45 often have difficulties obtaining a first mortgage. You should also note that in some parts of France, such as the Riviera, there is a substantial shortage of properties available to rent.

On balance, however, in my opinion you should rent for a period of at least six months or a year. In addition to enabling you to familiarise yourself with the area (and any major new developments in the pipeline, such as new motorway routes etc) it gives you the time to shop around and the ability to act quickly should a good opportunity become available.

Do not rush into signing a rental contract for a property that you have not seen before you arrive in France. It is advisable instead to find accommodation for a few weeks only, and then look around for a longer-term rental.

Finding a property to rent

The last couple of years have seen a substantial increase in the number of properties being advertised and let via the Internet, and many people now locate a property to rent this way. The largest French site is www.seloger.com. The sites www.explorimmo.com, and www.pap.fr are also worth visiting. Other sites include www.foncia.com, www.fnaim.fr, www.century21.fr and www.hestia.fr. The advantages of searching the Internet are considerable, in terms of choice, and the costs and time spent searching. Frequently you are provided with photographs of the premises, and plans showing its position in relation to local amenities. This can save a number of wasted time-consuming visits to properties that are clearly not within your requirements. On www.explorimmo.com you will find that the advertisements from the main national and regional newspapers (including *Le Figaro and Le Monde*) appear from six a.m., even before you can purchase a copy of the paper itself.

In addition to the main national and regional newspapers, it is well worth looking in the free newspaper that is circulated in each department, and which is known by its department number (in the Alpes-Maritimes, for example, it is known as the 06 – *le zéro six*). Try the English language media, including the growing number of anglophone web sites about France, where you will find a good selection of properties available to rent, in many cases owned by other British people who have purchased a holiday or retirement home in France. You will also find notices in the windows of shops, including those serving the English-speaking communities in France. Consider consulting the notice boards at the British Council, and in many of the churches with international congregations.

You should note that some of the properties advertised in newspapers do not exist. Some agents put in an advertisement for a property at an attractive rental simply in order to encourage readers to telephone them. They are fairly easy to detect however, as they will generally refuse to post information to you, avoid discussing details over the telephone, and insist that you attend their office to register. They charge a fee of around €150 – 200 and agree to show you round properties that come on their books that fit your requirements. If this works, you pay rather less commission than you would to a traditional agent (see below). In many cases, however, they have no suitable properties currently on their books, and you may have some wait before they do.

In addition you can contact estate agents (*agents immobiliers*) many of whom handle rental properties. You can obtain a list of these for your area from the local *bureau de tourisme* or from *les Pages Jaunes*. Estate agents charge both the tenant and the landlord one month's rental (plus TVA) each. In rural areas especially, it is worth contacting the local *notaires* to see if they have any clients with properties to rent. Their commission rates are lower than those charged by estate agents. If you are looking for an apartment, consider contacting several *administrateurs de biens* – essentially agents who manage blocks of flats and who often act for flat owners wishing to rent out their apartment.

Inspecting properties

Whilst you may not intend to stay long in the rental property that you are looking for, it is nevertheless going to be your home for a few months, and perhaps for longer than you initially anticipated. Accordingly I strongly recommend that you visit it at least twice, ideally at completely different times of the day. If at all possible, introduce yourself to the occupiers of neighbouring properties. According to several French documentaries that I have seen, neighbour disputes are a major problem in France. Especially if you are renting an apartment, a noisy and aggressive neighbour can prove a major problem. One short "hello" may be enough to realise that the property is best avoided.

If you will be in the property during the day, perhaps with children, working or sleeping if you work unsocial hours, watch out for any indications that building works are or may be about to take place nearby. When visiting a property, be sure to determine what will be left by the existing occupiers – in France most longer term rentals are unfurnished, and unfurnished can mean without carpets and curtains, kitchen and sink units or even light fittings.

Landlords' requirements

The landlord or his agent will wish to see your most recent salary slips, and if you are already renting ask to see your present rental agreement. In the past many landlords insisted that tenants should have an income four times the rental level, though most now accept tenants with incomes at only three times the rent, and some will accept incomes less than this. He will also require a deposit (*caution*) and often a guarantee (see below).

Protection for tenants under French law

A tenant in France benefits from a considerably greater level of protection than is currently the case in the UK, especially when it comes to his rights to stay in the property. The laws protecting tenants apply irrespective of what is contained in the written rental agreement between the landlord and the tenant. They apply even if the agreement is in English and between English speaking landlords and tenants, and even if the rental contract was agreed and signed in the UK, or anywhere else for that matter. Note that the legislation that protects tenants does not extend to seasonal lettings (*les locations saisonnières*) or second residences (*les résidences secondaires*). Until recently non-seasonal lettings of furnished properties were also unprotected, though that has now changed (see on). The sections below relate primarily to standard non-furnished rentals, but much of the advice applies also to the renting of furnished premises.

The rental agreement (le contrat de bail)

This is a document that sets out your liabilities, as well as your rights, and accordingly you should read this through with some care. It is a legal document and many French people would not find this an easy task. You should therefore obtain assistance from someone who is familiar with rental agreements and speaks a high level of French, or seek the advice of a *notaire* or avocat who speaks English well. Many of those who claim or believe that they can speak English do not do so to a sufficiently high level.

A tenancy contract can be oral, but I strongly recommend that you obtain a written contract. This should state the names of the proprietor (*le propriétaire*) and the tenant (*le locataire*), the start date and length of the tenancy. It should contain a description of the property, and set out the level of rent, the amount of the deposit and the use for which the property is being let. If for some reason you do not have a written contract, you have a right to be provided with this on request (see the draft letter at the end of this chapter).

Under French law a spouse is automatically a tenant also, irrespective of whether the marriage took place before or after the signing of a tenancy agreement. Accordingly a spouse has the same rights, and the same obligation as his or her partner.

The deposit and guarantee

You will generally be required to pay a deposit of two month's rent before moving into the property, as a guarantee that you will keep the property in a good condition. Some proprietors will sometimes accept part payment, with the balance to be paid a month or two after the tenant has moved in.

In many cases assistance is available to those with difficulties in providing a deposit and or guarantee. *The LocaPass* gives the landlord security by providing him with the full value of the deposit, which the tenant refunds by monthly instalments. The landlord also receives a rental guarantee of up to 18 months over the first three years' rental. *The*

LocaPass is available to those under 30 in salaried employment or seeking salaried employment, and students in receipt of a state *bourse* (grant). *The LocaPass* is administered at a local level. You can find out which body administers it in your locality by consulting the UESL (*L'Union d'Economie Sociale pour le Logement*) on 01 44 858100, or on its web site www.uesl.fr or by consulting any of the tenants' rights organisations listed later in this chapter or in front of *Les Pages Jaunes*.

A landlord may request payment of rent every three months. A tenant has the right, however, to chose to pay monthly. If rent is paid on a three basis, then the landlord has no right to insist on a deposit.

At the end of the rental, the landlord has two months in which to repay the deposit (without interest) to the tenant. The landlord can deduct his costs of rectifying any damage to the property and any unpaid rent. The landlord is required to pay interest on the deposit should he retain it for longer than two months. If you have difficulties recovering your deposit, then you should send a *lettre recommandée avec avis de réception* to your landlord. The post office will send you a notification that the letter has (or has not) been received. If you have not received reimbursement of the deposit within eight days from the date the landlord received your letter, then you are entitled to take court proceedings to recover it. You should seek advice from an *avocat* or one of the various tenants' organisations listed below.

The level of rent

In theory a landlord is restricted in the rent he can require a new tenant to pay – if he cannot reach agreement with a prospective tenant then the parties will have to apply to the *Tribunal d'Instance*. In practice, where there is a shortage of properties, the landlord will look for another tenant. On the other hand, a landlord is only able to increase the rent of an existing tenant if he can justify it by a comparison with the rentals of other properties. He is required to send a recorded delivery letter to the tenant six months prior to the end of the existing tenancy stating his proposal for the new level of rent and enclosing details of three other similar properties in the locality (six in Paris, Marseille and Lyon). If the tenant does not accept the landlord's figure, the landlord must apply to the local *Commission de Conciliation*. If still no agreement can be reached, the landlord must apply to the *Tribunal d'Instance*.

The duration of the tenancy agreement

Under French law, subject to certain exceptions (see below), a tenancy must be for a minimum of three or six years, depending upon the type of landlord. The minimum period is three years if the landlord is a private individual (*un particulier*) or a *Société Civile Immobilière*. The latter is a company specifically set up to own and manage rental properties, and the letters SCI will appear after its name. The minimum period is six years if the landlord is a *personne morale* i.e. a bank or insurance company.

A tenant is entitled to terminate the tenancy before the end of the three / six year period, but cannot be required to leave his home before the end of the agreement unless he has breached a significant term of the contract, for example when he has failed to pay his rent, caused damage to the property, sublet the property without the landlord's consent, or disturbed neighbours. A landlord is always required to obtain a court order before he is entitled to evict a tenant. This can take some time, and a tenant will normally be given the opportunity to remedy his breach of the agreement. A tenant in arrears with his rent will generally be given time to pay. He will usually have to be several months in arrears before a landlord is able to obtain a court order for possession of the property.

Furthermore, a tenant has an automatic right to extend the tenancy for a further three years (or six years if his landlord is a bank or insurance company). A landlord is obliged to accept such a request for renewal unless he wishes to live in it himself (or requires it for certain close family members), the tenant has significantly breached the tenancy agreement or he wishes to sell it. If the landlord wishes to sell, the tenant has the right of first refusal. If nothing is decided but the tenant remains in occupation of the property, then the tenancy is automatically renewed for a further three or six years.

The government has provided for additional protection for tenants of flats owned by banks and insurance companies that decide to sell more than 10 dwellings in a block of flats. In brief, when such a landlord wants possession of an apartment where the tenant's income is below €66,000 per year he must provide suggestions for alternative accommodation. For those who are infirm or aged over 75 but not paying wealth tax, their tenancies are automatically renewed. All tenants who have lived in the property for more than six years receive an extension to their tenancy of one month per year of occupancy, up to a maximum of an additional 30 months.

Shorter tenancies

A landlord is entitled to rent the property for a shorter period than the three years, but only if he can show that he has a specific family or work reason for needing to do so. Permitted reasons include going to work abroad for a year and wishing to live in the property on his return, or because of a planned marriage. The proprietor must specify the reason why he will need the property back before he grants the tenancy, and the tenancy must still be for at least twelve months. Furthermore, the landlord is required to send a recorded delivery notification to the tenant, at least two months before the end of the tenancy, confirming that the he still requires the property for the reason specified at the outset. If the landlord does not send such a notice, then the tenancy will convert into the standard three-year tenancy.

Maintenance, repairs, charges and improvements

A tenant is responsible for carrying out minor repairs, and carrying out basic maintenance to keep the property in a good state of repair. This covers replacing broken windows, broken keys, paintwork, bleeding of radiators, replacement of bulbs, fuses and light fittings. Substantial works of maintenance and repair remain the responsibility of the landlord. A tenant is entitled to carry out minor works, for example, laying a carpet in an unfurnished property. A landlord's prior written consent is required before engaging in any significant work, including making holes in walls. A landlord has a right to carry out works of maintenance and improvement to the property. You may well find that the proprietor decides to carry out substantial building works that cause you considerable disturbance, and from which you may never benefit! Accordingly, especially if you intend to rent for a short period only, and/or are going to spent a lot of time in the property during working hours, it is worthwhile asking for the landlord to confirm in writing that he (or his successor, if he sells) will not carry out any works of improvement whilst you are in occupation without your consent. Ask for this to be noted on the tenancy contract, and the addition signed and dated.

Whilst a landlord is entitled to recover any expenditure that he incurs on behalf of the tenant, for example in relation to basic maintenance of the property, or the costs of heating and lighting, a tenant is entitled to proof of the expenditure, although he has one month only from receiving the landlord's account in which to challenge it.

Restrictions imposed on landlords

Landlords regularly attempt to impose requirements on tenants. The law, however, forbids them from:

- requiring rent to be paid by direct debit or from a tenant's salary
- preventing a tenant from keeping a pet (although they have been allowed to ban pit bulls and other dangerous pets)
- insisting that the tenant chose a particular insurance company to insure the property
- preventing a tenant from working from home

A tenant's right to work from home

A landlord cannot prevent a tenant from working from a residential rental providing the property is the tenant's sole or principal residence, and providing he does not receive clients or merchandise at the property. The rules are relaxed somewhat for childminders.

In apartment blocks however, a tenant is also subject to the same rules and regulations that govern all the occupiers, including those who own their apartments. These often restrict the right to use the premises for work purposes.

Other matters

Rental agreements often require a tenant to take out an insurance policy to start as soon as he is handed the keys. A landlord may be entitled to withdraw from the rental agreement unless this is done. He is entitled to request proof of insurance. A tenant has no right to sublet a rented property unless he has his landlord's permission, which should be in writing. Even if he sublets with his landlord's permission, he is still liable to pay rent to his landlord, even if his sub-tenant stops paying rent. Do not accept a sub-tenancy unless you have the written consent of the owner of the property. It is better, however, to have a direct tenancy agreement with the proprietor.

Recording the condition of the property before you move in and when you leave

It is normal to have an *"Etat des Lieux"* carried out before a tenant moves into the property. This is a record of the condition of the property at the time that the tenancy starts. In French law, a rented property is assumed to be in a good condition at the beginning of a tenancy, unless there is evidence to the contrary. As a tenant is required to return the property to the landlord in the same condition (subject to usual wear and tear), it is essential to record any defects prior to going into occupation, to avoid the possibility of the landlord later blaming you for defects that were already present in the property before you moved in.

An *Etat des Lieux* is frequently carried out by a *huissier*, who will carry out an inspection of the property before the tenant moves in, in the presence of the tenant and the landlord or his representative. This costs in the region of €235 – 300 and is split equally between the landlord and the tenant. It is advisable for a tenant to inspect the property himself before the *huissier* attends, and to make his own checklist of those matters he thinks should be mentioned by the *huissier*. I have included a suitable checklist at the end of this chapter. You can then mention the points that you have listed to the *huissier* at his inspection.

There is no obligation to have a *huissier*. You could attend at the property (perhaps with a friend) and prepare the *Etat des Lieux* with the landlord or his representative. Again, you could use the model at the end of this chapter. The *Etat des Lieux* should be completed in duplicate, and each signed by both parties.

The landlord may also supply you with an inventory covering any contents. Again, you should check that the inventory is correct before signing it. If you do notice inaccuracies in the inventory or the checklist of the condition of the property, you should send a recorded delivery letter to the landlord or his agent informing them as soon as possible.

It is also advisable to take a video showing the condition of the property when you move in. Ensure that you cover the entire property, and hone in on any defects, especially those that you feel were perhaps not recorded sufficiently on the *Etat des Lieux* or which you only notice whilst making the recording. Ensure that you can prove the date that the video was taken, perhaps by posting the video to yourself by recorded delivery and keeping the package unopened until you need it, at which time it should only be opened in front of a your *avocat*, or some other person who can confirm the date that it was opened, and that the package had not previously been opened.

Immediately after you have left the premises, a further *Etat des Lieux* must be carried out, and compared with that prepared prior to your entry into the property. Again, it is advisable to take another video, preferably after your possessions have been taken out. The video should include a recording of a news item on the television (or radio) so that there can be no suggestion that the video was carried out earlier.

Giving notice to leave

A tenant is permitted to give notice (*le congé*) to the landlord at any time during the tenancy. He must usually give three months' notice. The notice must either be sent to the landlord by *lettre recommandée avec avis de réception* or be delivered personally by a *huissier*. The three months starts to run on the date that the landlord receives the letter. This may be the day after it is posted if the postman is able to hand this to the landlord, otherwise the postman will leave a notice telling the landlord that there is a registered letter for him for collection at the post-office, in which case the three month period will not start to run until the letter is collected by the landlord. The post-office will send you a notification stating whether or not it has been delivered to the landlord.

A tenant is entitled to give his landlord only one month's notice where:

- he loses his job, or obtains a new job after losing his previous employment, or simply changes job
- he is older than 60 and he needs to move for health reasons
- his income is below a certain level

The requirements for giving notice are identical to those set out above for a three month notice period, save that the tenant must include documentary proof of his entitlement to give only one month's notice. If the tenant fails to do this, he will be held to the standard notice period, and will remain liable for the rent for three months.

There is a model letter for giving notice later in this chapter.

Note that if you leave before the end of a notice period, you remain liable for the rent, and are still responsible for the property and for keeping to the terms of the rental contract until the notice expires. If a tenant is able to find a new tenant for the property who is acceptable to the landlord then he can reduce this liability.

Furnished tenancies

Until recently there were very few restrictions relating to furnished tenancies. New legislation now provides tenants of furnished properties with substantial protection. Where furnished premises are a tenant's principal residence, the contract must be for at least twelve months. Furthermore, if the landlord wishes to obtain possession at the end of the year, he must serve notice on the tenant at least three months before the expiry of the tenancy. If he gives no notice, or only late notice, then the tenancy is renewed automatically for a further twelve months. Even if the landlord gives the correct notice there are substantial restrictions on his right to recover possession. A tenant, on the other hand, is only obliged to give one month's notice, and this can be at any time. In brief, renting out a property with furniture in it is no longer such an attractive alternative for a landlord compared to letting a property unfurnished.

Disagreements with your landlord

If your landlord is harassing you, or failing to comply with his obligation to carry out repairs, or is refusing to return the deposit to you, then you should contact one of the tenants' associations referred to below which can provide you with initial advice without charge. One excellent option is to take out a legal expenses policy with your insurer at the beginning of the tenancy. The policy normally entitles you to telephone the insurer's lawyer for preliminary advice (on a wide range of issues, not just renting), and some policies will cover some or all of your legal costs in litigation, including against the landlord (for example, in relation to recovering your deposit). To instruct a lawyer without such a policy can be expensive, and may be out of proportion to the amount that you are owed.

Litigation can be avoided by making use of the free voluntary conciliation procedure (*la conciliation judiciaire*). To invoke this procedure you have to write to *le greffe du Tribunal d'Instance* setting out the main points of the dispute. Each side puts it case to the judge, who then states his opinion. The parties are not bound by the judge's finings.

Right of first refusal

A tenant of a long-term letting is entitled to first refusal should the proprietor put the property up for sale (this is referred to as *le droit de préemption*). The landlord should notify you, in writing, of the sale price, and the conditions of sale. If the landlord fails to do this, the tenant has the right to have the sale annulled, and to purchase the property at the price recorded on the contract for sale.

Further information on renting or advice on problems with renting

L'Agence Nationale pour l'Information sur le Logement, 2, bd Saint-Martin 75010 (tel: 01.42.02.50.50). This organisation has a very informative web site www.anil.org, with useful information for tenants (and landlords), including details of the new laws governing the letting of furnished properties. Other sources of assistance include:

La Confédération du logement et du cadre de vie (CLCV): tel: 01 56 54 32100. Web site: www.clcv.org)

L'Association des Comités de Défense des Locataires (ACDL) 11, rue de Bellefond, 75009 Paris (Tel: 01 48 74 94 84).

La Direction Departementale de l'Equipement (DDE) and

L'Association Départementale pour l'Information sur le Logement (ADIL) also provide location information. For the latter see under *ADIL* in the section of the *Les Pages Blanches for your locality*.

Etat des lieux

Entre .... (Locataire)
et .... (propriétaire)

Adresse du logement loué: ....

Date d'entrée: ....

I = excellent   2 = bon   3 = passable   4 = mauvais

pièce	peinture plafond vitrerie	sol portes fenêtres stores	electricité	rangements	plomberie sanitaires	serrurerie
Séjour						
Cuisine						
Chambre I						
Chambre 2						
Chambre 3						
Salle de bains						
Toiletttes						
Entrée						
Cave						
Garage						

(Signed)   Le locataire   le propriétaire

Etat des lieux

Between .... (Tenant)
and .... (Landlord)

Address of rented property: ....

Date of commencement of occupation: ....

1 = excellent   2 = good   3 = passable   4 = poor

room	paintwork ceiling window-panes	floor doors windows blinds	electricity	cupboards/ storage units	plumbing ironworks	locks
Living room						
Kitchen						
Bed 1						
Bed 2						
Bed 3						
Toilet						
Bathroom						
Hall/ entrance way						
Cellar						
Garage						

(signed)   Tenant :   Landlord :

TENANTS' LETTER GIVING NOTICE OF TERMINATION
(congé de la part des locataires)
Your name
Your address

> Name of proprietor
> Proprietor's address

Date (e.g. vendredi 25 janvier 20 ..)
Recommandée A. R.

Monsieur et/ou Madame,

Dear Sir and/or Madam,

Nous vous délivrons, par la présente, congé pour le 30 avril du logement que nous occupons et que nous louons en vertu d'un contrat de location conclu le

We hereby give you notice of termination for 30th April in relation to the rental premise that we occupy that we rent under an agreement dated the

Nous vous précisons qu'il conviendra de dresser un état des lieux lors de la restitution du logement.

We consider that an état des lieux should be drawn up once the premises are vacated.

Nous nous permettons de vous rappeler que vous devez nous restituer le montant du dépôt de garantie que nous vous avons versé, soit €.

We would remind you that you should return the deposit to us that we gave you, namely €.

Veuillez agréer, Monsieur et/ou Madame, l'expression de nos sentiments les meilleurs.

Yours sincerely,

Should you be entitled to give one month's notice, the first paragraph should be replaced with the following :
«Nous sommes locataires de (put address) *que nous louons en vertu*

d'un contrat de location conclu le . Nous avons l'honneur, par la présente, de vous délivrer congé d'un mois, suite à : (choose the appropriate reason)

une perte d'emploi
(loss of a job)

un nouvel emploi trouvé consécutif à la perte d'un précédent emploi
(a new job following the loss of a previous job)

une mutation par mon employeur dans une autre ville
(transfer by employer to a new location)

j'ai plus de soixante ans, et j'ai besoin de changer de domicile pour ma santé »
(more than 60 and need to change house for reasons of health)

Buying a Property in France

For most people, the purchase of a home in France has proved a sound long-term investment. The purchase of a property abroad, however, can result in serious financial losses and in some cases lengthy and difficult court proceedings. The peaceful holiday or retirement home (or worse still your main residence) can turn into a veritable nightmare. You will find comprehensive advice on buying property in France (and also on letting out your French property) in my book *The Complete Guide to Buying Property in France* published by Kogan Page. I have set out below a short set of basic guidelines.

If you decide to purchase in France you should bear the following in mind:

- *do not expect to obtain a quick short term capital gain.* In France the acquisition costs are high. It is safest to work on the basis that you will need to own your property for several years before you will make a net gain on any sale;

- *instruct your own lawyer.* French *notaires* are publicly appointed officials. Their main functions are to draft legal documents, to oversee the transfer of property, to inform the parties of their tax liabilities, and to ensure that monies have been paid. They are not representing your interests. Specifically they do not carry out the important pre-contract enquiries that, for example, a solicitor in the UK would carry out. Chose a lawyer, or a team of lawyers, who can communicate well in a language that you can fully understand, and secondly who have an understanding of inheritance and tax law in the UK, as well as in France. The earlier you instruct your lawyer the better;

- *get to know the area in which you wish to purchase.* Familiarise yourself with the climate - much of France has a continental climate – stiflingly hot in summer and bitterly cold in winter. Ascertain whether the area suffers from natural disasters. Some areas are subject to flooding. There is no need automatically to exclude these areas, but take special care when making enquiries as to the particular property and surrounding area;

- *obtain a surveyor's report.* Lending institutions in France generally require only a valuation. A structural survey prevents you from purchasing a property that is structurally unsound, perhaps dangerous, expensive to restore and difficult to sell. In addition, a report often identifies non-structural defects that may not deter you from your purchase, but may give you ammunition to negotiate on the purchase price;

- *view the property yourself.* Ideally you should visit the property several times, at different times of the day, and in different weather conditions. Approach the property from different routes. Try to ascertain why the vendors are selling, and if at all possible speak to the neighbours. Look to see if the boundaries to the property are clearly marked. Is there any evidence of any rights of way being used over the property? Inform your surveyor and lawyer of any concerns you have – your surveyor will probably only visit once, and your lawyer not at all;

- *do not declare at an undervalue:* the authorities in France have tightened up on the rules, and are likely to become even stricter in the future. If you under declare you risk a much larger capital gain and hence higher tax bill when you come to sell. Furthermore, if the authorities are not happy with the amounts declared they can (and do) have the property valued and impose penalties on both buyer and seller.

Chapter Three

FINDING A JOB IN FRANCE

As a citizen of the European Union you are entitled to live and work anywhere within the European Union. There are no formalities required to search for employment in France, other than the possession of a valid passport. However, unemployment is higher in France than the UK, though there is a shortage of labour in certain sectors, notably in IT.

The French Labour Market

As a foreigner you are already at some disadvantage in approaching French employers even if you speak French to a high level. Furthermore, in recent years there has been considerable immigration into France, primarily economic migrants especially from Portugal, Spain, and North Africa seeking unskilled or semi-skilled work. You should not assume that finding employment will be straightforward. Do not assume that you will walk into a post teaching English. The French employ very few British nationals to teach English in their schools. They also have a strong preference for fellow French nationals when it comes to private English lessons. There are, of course, quite a number of posts available as English language assistants, but foreign assistants are considerably less well paid than professional teachers, and the contract generally only covers October to May (see on). A teaching qualification, especially the PGCE (Post Graduate Certificate in Education), or a TEFL (Teaching English as a Foreign Language) qualification, will increase your chances of finding work, though earnings are generally quite low. If you wish to teach English, then your prospects of making a living will be much higher in Spain, where there are far more English language courses.

Unemployment benefit

If you are unemployed in the UK and have been registered as a job seeker for at least four weeks, you can arrange for Jobseeker's Allowance to be paid to you in France for up to 13 weeks. You must remain available for work until you leave, and the reason for your departure must be to search for work. You are required to register as seeking work with the French authorities within seven days of your last claim for Jobseeker's Allowance in the UK. You should make enquiries at your local Jobcentre Plus office or Jobcentre to complete the appropriate forms. In particular, you should obtain leaflet JSAL 22. You should also be given an E303 and an E119 before leaving. The former is to allow you to claim benefit in France. The latter establishes your entitlement to health care in France. If you are not successful in finding work during that 13-week period, then you will cease to be entitled to receive Job Seeker's Allowance unless you return to the UK. If you obtain a job in the UK, but then are unemployed again, you can receive a further 13-weeks of the allowance whilst searching for employment in France, or elsewhere in the EU. Information on transferring your Job Seeker's Allowance is contained in leaflet JSAL 22 available from your local DWP office. See Chapter 7 for further information on receiving UK benefits whilst in France.

In France the payment of unemployment benefit is handled by *L'Association pour l'Emploi Dans l'Industrie et le Commerce (ASSEDIC)*. Payment is monthly. The web site is at www.assedic.fr.

Finding employment

A great many English speakers find employment within the anglophone community in France, particularly on the Riviera, in the tourist industry, the yachting industry, security services, childcare and as domestic staff. A large number of expatriates find and keep such employment without speaking or learning French at all. However, if you wish to have any realistic prospects of obtaining employment with a French employer, you need to have a reasonable knowledge of French and a willingness to improve it. You will find below the main resources available to assist you in your search for work.

Different forms of employment contracts

There are several different forms of contract that employers can offer, including contracts in which they receive funding or financial incentives from the state, for example in relation to taking on trainees, those who have been unemployed for more than twelve months etc. Further details are contained in Chapter 4. The government also provides state aid to employees to aid geographical mobility. If you accept a new job, either a permanent position, or a fixed term contract of at least twelve months that is more than 25 km from your home, or that requires more than one hour to get to work, you are entitled to a payment of up to €1,916 (*L'Aide à la mobilité géographique*). This is tax-free and is not subject to social security contributions.

EURES (European Employment Service)

The European Commission sees greater mobility of labour as a key factor in the economic growth of the EU and for promoting political integration within the EU. It has set up a co-operation network to liase with the national employment services of member states, to encourage free movement of workers. EURES seeks to ascertain where there are shortages of labour, and how these can be met. It also has the task of promoting the proper recognition of qualifications by the various member states.

Once you have decided to seek employment, or indeed to study, in France you should contact EURES. It is an invaluable source of information and advice about living and working in France and can assist you in obtaining employment. There is no charge for this service. Start by browsing the EURES website www.europa.eu.int/jobs/eures and considering the job offers listed at www.eures-jobs.com. The latter is regularly up-dated, and you can search by professions and regions. EURES is in the process of making all posts advertised by member states' public employment services accessible from this site. Those posts where the employer has expressed particular interest in taking on workers from other EU countries are marked with a blue flag. The EURES site also permits you to create a CV and make it available to employers, and to EURES advisers.

In addition to consulting the site, you should contact your local EURES adviser through your local Jobcentre Plus office. His or her job is to provide advice and assistance to job seekers and employers, and he should put you in contact with the EURES adviser in the region in France in which you wish to work. Another useful source of information and assistance is the interactive programme *On the Move* that is accessible via www.europa.eu.int. Go to the Ploteus Portal and then "links".

L'Agence National pour L'Emploi (ANPE)

Those seeking employment in France should register in person with their local office of ANPE, which is the same office at which you are required to register if you are to have UK Job Seekers Allowance paid to you in France. All EU citizens are entitled to the same level of help and assistance as a French citizen. This can include not only help in finding employment, but also assistance in selecting appropriate training courses (*la formation*), and advice on setting up your own business. On a practical level you will be provided with access to a telephone booth from which you can telephone prospective employers without charge, to a computer to prepare your CV, to the Internet and to a photocopier. The larger centres also contain useful reference books and material. ANPE offices are listed in *Les Pages Jaunes* under *Administration du Travail et de l'Emploi*. At your first interview at ANPE the adviser will prepare with you a *Projet d'Action Personalisé (PAP)* – a plan of action designed to assist you in your search for employment. Job advertisements in the French media, or at the equivalent to a Jobcentre in the UK (the ANPE) often refer to *Bac*, or *Bac +2, or Bac +3*. Bac is a reference to the French baccalauréat, an examination taken at around age 18. The addition of a figure is to indicate that applicants must have at least that number of years of higher education.

Employment Agencies (temporary work)

There are many temporary employment agencies in France. They are listed under *Intérim* in the Yellow Pages. Some of the largest include Manpower (www.manpower.fr), Adecco (www.adecco.fr), Kelly Service (www.kellyservices.fr), ADIA France (www.adia.fr), Best-Intérim (www.best-interim.fr), E-Boss (www.e-boss.fr), ISA Intérim (www.isa-interim.com covering hotels, restaurants and the building trade) and Quick Médical Service (www.interim-medical.com). You should consider making contact with such recruitment agencies, sending a CV and covering letter and requesting an appointment to see them. It may also be worth contacting *Manpower* in the UK before leaving (0207 224 66 88) and also consulting the web site www.officielinterim.com.

The various agencies cover a wide range of different employments, including management positions. A temporary post may often lead directly to a permanent appointment, or provide you with the experience you need to add to your Curriculum Vitae, or the reference that you will require to apply for a permanent post. Temporary workers should receive the same benefits as a permanent worker, including the 13th month salary, lunch vouchers and traffic subsidies. At the end of the temporary contract you should receive a payment equivalent to 10% of the gross salary that you have earned, plus an amount to cover paid holidays not taken.

The Media

Scan the classified ads in *Le Figaro* (Mondays), and for higher paid jobs *Le Monde* (Mondays and Tuesdays) as well as specialist magazines such as *Carrières et Emplois* (Wednesdays) and regional newspapers. Salaries are seldom indicated in advertisements. In addition there are many English language newspapers, magazines and web sites for the Anglophone community in France that are increasingly containing job advertisements. In Paris these include *Free Voice* and *France-USA Contacts*. You will find details of other local English language publications in Appendix 1 and in the different regional sections in Chapter 1. English language radio stations, such as Riviera Radio (www.rivieraradio.mc) often have job spots.

Job placements

Those who have only recently joined the job market may succeed in obtaining a traineeship or job placement in France with one of the larger multi-national employers (e.g. Unilever – www.you-unilever.com). This is an ideal opportunity to improve your French, experience life in France and assess your future prospects in France. If you are a student you may benefit from one of the work experience programmes. Details of many of theses can be obtained from The International Association for the Exchange of Students for Technical Experience (IAESTE), The Educational and Training Group, The British Council, 10 Spring Gardens, London SW1 2BN (tel 0207 389 4774, e-mail iaeste@britishcouncil.org, website www.iaeste.org.uk). In addition the EU has schemes such as Europass and the Leonardo da Vinci programme that enable young people to carry out vocational training in other member states. A useful starting point is the British Council's "Windows of the World" site at www.wofw.org.uk

Networking

In Paris, and other areas with large numbers of British expatriates, your prospects of obtaining employment may be substantially increased if you participate in ex-pat life, especially if you speak little or no French. Networking enables you to find out about vacancies that may not be advertised, and is also extremely important if you wish to set up and run your own business. Read the local anglophone newspapers and magazines and consult their web sites, and the sites of American and British Chambers of Commerce (see Appendix 1) on some of which you can place an advertisement setting out your qualifications and experience. Other options include notices on the notice boards of expatriate organisations, clubs and associations, shops, bars and even churches frequented by other English speakers.

Unsolicited letters of application

A surprising number of people obtain employment by sending unsolicited well-written letters (*lettres de motivation*) and CVs to a wisely chosen selection of companies. You should find out as much as you can about a company before you write, and compose your letter with their likely requirements in mind. Always check the company's website, for information about the company, and to see whether they have a facility to submit an application by e-mail, and if they have a standard application form. Even if you decide not to use the company's standard form, at least take on board the sort of questions contained on the form, and which you are likely to be asked at some point. You can obtain a list of American companies operating in France in the trade directory and international database for France (costing around €90) available from any American Chamber of Commerce or from www.americansabroad.com. French directories of businesses include Kompass, accessible on www.kompass.fr. Two other useful sites with directories are www.bottin.fr and www.europages.com. Information about particular businesses can be found on www.euridile.inpi.fr. For letters in French it is worthwhile purchasing a specialist book on how to present different types of CVs and how to address and set out your correspondence. These are often sold in the larger supermarkets.

Your covering letter should be brief and to the point, hand written and in perfect French. It should include a summary of your qualifications and experience and state why you have chosen to seek employment with that particular company, and indicate the strongest points in your favour. Always use a white envelope, and attach the letter to your CV with a paper clip. Do not forget to include an international reply coupon if writing from outside France, as well as a self-addressed envelope. It is important to appreciate that French business correspondence is more formal than in the UK, and you *must* follow a standard style. Always begin your letter with a formal opening such as *Monsieur, Madame, Monsieur le Directeur* or *Madame la Directrice*. The ending should be likewise formal, such as *Veuillez agréer, Monsieur le Directeur, l'expression de mes sentiments distingués* ("yours faithfully"), followed by your signature (with your name typed underneath). Your curriculum vitae must be well structured, clear and concise. Compose each CV separately by adapting your standard CV to appeal to the particular employer. If you cannot fit your CV onto to two typed pages of A4 papers (without crowding the pages), then your CV is almost certainly too long. Always use good quality white paper, and include a translation if it is not written in French.

A useful starting point for the preparation of your CV is the EU's European Standard Curriculum Vitae. It is available in 13 languages and can be downloaded via the EURES website www.europa.eu.int/jobs/eures. Photographs, qualifications and references should not be sent with your CV, unless they have been requested.

Divide your CV into sections. You should start with personal details i.e. full name, date of birth, address and contact details, then have a second section setting out brief details and dates of your educational and training history, with separate paragraphs for IT and foreign language training. The third section should cover your work experience. Always start with your most recent employment. Include the names of your present and former employers, dates employed and nature of job carried out. A fourth section can be included dealing with any information that you consider particularly pertinent to your application, such as a clean driving licence.

Job interviews *(Entretiens d'embauche)*

You should already have obtained some information about your potential employer before you made your application or submitted your unsolicited CV. Once you obtain an invitation to attend for interview, take the time and trouble to find out more. Ensure that you are familiar with the "specialist language" that you would be expected to use if you were working for this employer – the vocabulary that you will be using on a daily basis will differ considerably according to the sector in which you would be employed. Be extremely positive about France and the French! Do not run down your own country or your fellow nationals! You will need to have with you three or four copies of your CV in French, a translation of your degree and/or other qualifications, your passport and two passport photographs.

Employment near the French border

EURES also plays a key role in creating cross-border partnerships involving both trade unions, employer organisations, regional authorities and vocational training services, such as the cross-border partnership covering Kent, Belgium and the North East corner of France. In these border areas people often live in one country and work in another. They can obtain extremely helpful advice and assistance from the EURES advises in relation to the administrative, legal or tax complications that they often encounter on a daily basis (see www.europa.eu.int/eures).

Having your qualifications recognised

To obtain a high mobility of labour in Europe, it is imperative that employees can have their qualifications recognised Europe-wide. With this objective in mind the EU has set up a network of National Academic Recognition Information Centres (NARICs) throughout European Union. They provide advice and information to educational institutions, students, teachers and business in relation to the academic recognition of qualifications and periods of study in other member states. NARICs, however, do not have the power to recognise foreign qualifications, as this is usually left to the individual institutes of higher education. You should note that it can take as long as 12 months or even longer to obtain official recognition, and therefore you should start the process as early as possible. It is worthwhile taking a look at the web site www.enic-naric.net, where you will find further details and links to the French and British NARIC web sites.

The contact details and address relating to France are:
Mme Françoise Profit, directrice ENIC-NARIC France
Centre international d'études pédagogiques
International Centre for Pedagogic studies
ENIC-NARIC France CIEP 4 rue Danton 75006 Paris
Phone: +33 1 55 55 04 28 Fax: +33 1 55 55 00 39
E-mail: enic-naric@ciep.fr   www.ciep.fr/enic-naricfr/

The system of recognition of a qualification depends on whether the profession is regulated or not. Regulated professions are those to which access is restricted to those holding the required qualifications, such as law or medicine. Non-regulated professions are subject to a general system of recognition, based on the principle that a person fully qualified in one member state should have the freedom to exercise his or her occupation in all member states. Where there are differences between the training received in the UK and France, the French authorities can require that you take an aptitude test or that a period of work experience should be undertaken. You should contact the government department responsible for your particular occupation. For additional information contact ENIC-NARIC France at the above address. It has overall responsibility for the validation and recognition of qualifications in France pursuant to the various European Directives. You will need to provide a certified copy of your academic and professional qualification (with an official translation), along with a certified copy of your passport. There is a modest fee payable.

The British Council: www.britcoun.org/france also has information on education and equivalence of qualifications. In addition it is worthwhile taking a look at www.eurescv-search.com

Difficulties in exercising your rights as a European citizen.

France is rather slow to implement European directives – its record in this respect is three times worse than that of the UK. Accordingly, you may well encounter problems in exercising your rights as an EU citizen, especially in relation to the recognition of qualifications. Fortunately the European Commission has produced a guide (Dialogue with Citizens) to help those who encounter problems in exercising their rights to live, work, travel and study within the EU. It sets out how to challenge adverse decisions and explains how to obtain a remedy where the host state has not played by the correct rules. To access Dialogue with Citizens go to www.europa.eu.int, then to Ploteus Portal and then 777777links. In addition the EU has created SOLVIT, an official body to deal with failures of member states to implement European directives, with offices in all member states. You should contact the UK office, not that in France. Contact details are obtainable by telephoning 00 800 678 91011 or on the website www.europa.eu.int/solvit/site/centres/index_en.htm.

Discrimination in employment

In 2005 the French government announced its intention to reduce discrimination in the work place, primarily by putting pressure on the *partenaires sociaux* i.e. employers and unions, to introduce measures themselves, but also by requiring businesses to keep a record of the ethnic make-up of their staff. Suggestions that are presently under consideration include having an "anonymous" CV to improve ethnic candidates' access to a first interview.

Measures have been introduced in relation to the employment of handicapped persons in public services. In short, if handicapped employees do not represent 6% of a public institution's payroll by 2006 then a fine is payable. The money recovered is to be used to assist schools, *mairies* and *préfectures* to carry out works to their premises to improve accessibility for the handicapped. A new law also provides that public buildings must be made accessible to handicapped people, within a period of ten years.

New regulations are to be introduced in relation to pay inequalities between men and women – at present it is estimated that men receive remuneration 15% higher than women for the same level of work. It is anticipated that the government will require a major reduction in this within the next five years

Different job catorgories
Teaching

There are occasional job vacancies for qualified (and unqualified) teaching staff across a range of academic subjects in the various British, American and International Schools in France. An ability to speak French is not always a requirement. Often these posts are advertised on the website of *The Times Educational Supplement*, and also on the websites of The European Council of International Schools (Tel: 0730 268244) www.ecis.org. It is well worth also checking the individual schools' web sites from time to time. Other web sites worth exploring are www.education.guardian.co.uk, www.tefl.com, www.tesjobs.co.uk, www.developingteachers.com, www.eslemployment.com

Teaching English

There are a large number of language schools across France, with obviously a high concentration in Paris. Do not assume that it will be easy to obtain a post – the French, especially outside of Paris, tend to prefer their own, even when it comes to teaching English. This is especially true in relation to assisting in the preparation of French school and third level examinations, when the immediate primary objective is the passing of an examination, rather than fluency in English. The approach of French educational bodies to the learning of English is rather dull, with a very heavy emphasis on grammar and grammatical rules, rather than practical oral and written fluency. The French, rightly in most cases, do not believe that British people know what is required for students to pass their examinations. This may change in the coming years, as according to official studies they are one of the worst nations in Europe at learning English. You will find a list of language schools in each department's Yellow Pages under *Cours de Langues* and at www.pagesjaunes.fr.

Each year a large number of British graduates and undergraduate students work in France as language assistants, speaking English to the students, giving information about English speaking countries and assisting the English language teachers. Assistants, who are generally under 30, normally work about 12 hours a week, and receive a modest but reasonable level of remuneration (currently around €760 per month, after tax and social security contributions). Positions are available in some primary schools as well as secondary level institutions. Further information is available from Assistants Department, Central Bureau for Educational Visits and Exchanges Tel: 020 7486 5101. Most applicants apply from the UK. Those resident in France should contact the *Centre International d'Etudes Pédagogiques* (CIEP), see www.cief.fr and tel: 00 33 145076080.

The usual rate for private lessons is between €10 and €20 per hour.

Interpreters and translators

As trade between the UK and France continues to grow, and more and more British live and work in France, there is an increasing need for interpreters and translators. There is nevertheless considerable competition, and professional translators work hard to establish and keep a client base. The best-paid work is technical and legal translation, though this is often the most difficult, and rather dry. You can obtain information about working with languages from The Institute of Linguists (www.iol.org.uk). See also www.languagejobs.org. Within European institutions there is a considerable demand for translators and interpreters with high levels of skills. Details of posts can be found on the web site of the European Communities Personnel Selection Office (EPSO) www.europa.eu.int/epso.

Information Technology

If you speak fluent French, and have qualifications and experience in IT, you should find no difficulties in obtaining employment in France. This is a sector in which there is a shortage of experienced personnel. Many French nationals in the IT sector move to London to improve their skills, though many stay longer than they intended because of the considerably higher salary levels in the UK.

Secretarial and office work

Those with word processing experience and a high level of French are well positioned to find secretarial work, especially in Paris. Even if you are seeking work within the expatriate community, a good level of French will be required. A working knowledge of Italian is a substantial advantage on the Côte d'Azur. For bilingual and legal secretaries a good starting point (and perhaps finishing point), especially for posts in Paris, is Dorothy Danahy Legal (01 47 20 13 13; www.dorothydanahy.com) which includes a number of the larger UK law firms amongst its clients.

The Yachting Industry: recruitment and training

There is a substantial demand for yachting crew and personnel on the south coast of France. The main agencies for recruitment and training in the yachting industry include: YPI Crew (04 92 90 4610); Camper & Nicholson (www.cnconnect.com); Global Crew Network (00 44 77 73361959; www.globalcrewnetwork.com); Fred Dovaston (www.yachtjob.com); www.yachtingpages.com; and Viking Recruitment (00 44 1304 240881; www.vikingrecruitment.com). A very useful starting point is the Riviera Radio website www.rivieraradio.mc

Domestic Staff

Agencies include Fleurs de Provence that has a regular demand for housekeepers, personnel to carry out household repairs, catering staff, gardeners, nannies and cleaners. Tel: 04 93 34 60 73; www.fleursdeprovence.com. Another agency, again in the south of France, is Oasis Services, tel: 04 93 656123.

Nursing

See www.graduatenurse.com. There has been a substantial shortage of nurses in France, and the authorities have recently carried out a campaign to recruit nurses from Spain, where salaries are lower. There is a high demand for medical, nursing and health service staff during the summer (see below).

Working from home

Note that if you are able to work from home, you benefit from a 50% tax deduction. There is no tax at all to pay on the first 12,000 euros of earnings, and you receive a further 1,500 euros tax-free allowance per dependant. There are opportunities in such fields as telemarketing for those with telephone and Internet connections. For information see the web sites www.sosfres.fr, www.ipsos.co, www.bva.fr.

Summer and seasonal work

There is a wide range of summer jobs available in France (and in the ski resorts during the winter months). They include sports instructors (especially water sports), crew and service staff for yachts, courier work, hotel and restaurant staff, gardening, representatives for tour operators, bar work, shop assistants, fruit and grape picking. For many posts an ability to speak foreign languages is an advantage, and for others a clean driving licence or a qualification in first aid (*le brevet de secourisme*) can be important. There is a major shortage of labour on the Côte d'Azur over the summer, with around 300,000 temporary staff being recruited from mid-June to mid-September, to cater for the millions of tourists that visit the region. Earnings in the hotel and holiday industries remain low, and accommodation is expensive and often difficult to find. Those working in a hotel and receiving the minimum wage are entitled to the provision of two meals a day by their employer (or an additional payment in lieu). General websites that are worthwhile taking a look at are: www.overseasjob.com, www.eurosummerjobs.com, www.summerjobs.com, and www.resortjobs.com. A particularly useful book is *Summer Jobs Abroad* published by Vacation Work. French sites include www.jobalacarte.com, www.jobsaison.com, www.studyrama.com, www.adecco.fr and www.manpower.fr. Two French trade unions have produced useful guides on seasonal jobs: *Ma saison en poche: le guide des saisonniers* available from the *Conféderation Générale du Travail* (CGT), www.cgt.fr and Jobs et saisonniers: vos droits ne sont pas en vacances by the *Conféderation Française Démocratique du Travail* (CFDT), www.cdft.fr.

For the Côte d'Azur the ANPE and the Centre Régional Information Jeunesse have put together a guidebook for those seeking summer work. *Conseillers* from ANPE can be contacted on 04 93 97 90 00 from 9.00 a.m. to 4.30 p.m. Monday to Thursday and from 9.00 a.m. to 1.00 p.m. Friday, with an interactive telephone service outside those hours. Web sites to consult include www.anpe.fr and www.crij.org/nice. To obtain a copy of the guidebook, telephone the CRIJ in Nice on 04 93 80 9393. It contains extremely helpful information across a wide range of sectors including employment in hotels, restaurants, the leisure industry and agriculture (harvesting).

Some of the larger businesses that require additional staff over the summer include Carrefour, La Poste, SNCF (www.recrutement-sncf.com), and the larger banks. For shop work you will find lists of the larger hypermarkets and supermarkets in the Yellow Pages under *Centres Commerciaux et grands magasins and Supermarchés et hypermarchés*. Recruitment for summer jobs can start any time from January. For jobs in hotels and restaurants (including waiting on table, bar work, dish washing, kitchen assistants, chamber maids etc), see www.soshotellerie.com and www.lechef.com and also the weekly publication *Journal de l'Hôtellerie*, from early March. Seasonal contracts in this industry oblige the employer to include meals for their staff. Many candidates obtain employment by visiting prospective employers (avoid lunch-times and after 3.00 p.m.) after consulting a local edition of the Yellow Pages (under *Hôtels et Restaurants*).

During the summer months there is a huge demand for drivers and motorcycle riders, ranging from chauffeurs to bus drivers to pizza deliverymen and women. On the roads, there is a need to recruit temporary staff to work in the motorway network's service stations and tollbooths (for the latter see www.escota.fr). There is also a demand for leaflet distributors. The hours are usually flexible, though you may have to be over 18 and have a means of transport. For potential employers, see the Yellow pages under *Distribution d'imprimés*, or contact the offices of the local and free newspapers. Those who want to try their hand at telephone sales should contact the *Syndicat du marketing téléphonique et médias électroniques* (0892686872).

If you want to work in holiday centres with children and young adults your chances are substantially higher if you obtain a BAFA (*Brevet d'Aptitude aux Fonctions d'Animateur*). To obtain this you must be at least 17 and undergo training lasting four weeks, at a cost of between €700 and €900. Earnings are on average a modest €16.85 per day plus board and lodging. In some cases the local *Conseil Regional* or *Direction Regional Jeunesse et Sport* will fund this cost. If you wish to work in this sector on a regular basis there are various other qualifcations that you can obtain. Holiday centres also need to take on individuals with some medical or nursing training as *assistants sanitaires*, and those who have finished their first year of training are often eligible for these posts. For jobs in the tourist industry, consult the Yellow Pages under *Agences de Voyages, Campings, Tourisme*, and *Vacances*, and also consult the local *Mairies* in the various holiday resorts who take on numerous temporary staff during the summer months. Other useful contacts include: L'UCPA (*l'Union nationale des Centres sportifs de Plein Air*) – visit their site at www.ucpa.com and search under *Recrutement*); www.animjobs.com and www.zanimateurs-fous.com. One major employer is Club Med (www.clubmed-jobs.com).

Temporary nursing and medical staff, and ancilliary workers (ranging from hospital porters to cleaners, maintenance staff and kitchen personnel) are also in high demand during the summer, when peak demand for health services coincides with staff holidays. Information can be otbained from www.quickmedicalservice.fr.

There are numerous opportunities for child-minding, with most positions being filled via small notices in shop windows. Two sites that are worth looking at are www.aufeminin.com and www.mababysitter.com. The parents are required to accompany babysitters home after midnight, or to pay for a taxi. Rates usually range between €6.50 and €8 an hour.

In many parts of France large numbers of people are taken on in the agricultural sector during August and September to help with the harvest. This is demanding, and short-term work, seldom for more than four or five weeks. Information about recruitment can be found from the *Association Nationale pour l'Emploi et la Formation en Agriculture* (www.anefa.org), or by looking in the Yellow Pages under *Agriculture : approvisionnement et collecte, Arboriculture et production de fruits* and *Coopératives Agricoles*. Those working on the grape-picking harvest can expect to work around 8-9 hours per day, seven days a week for up to two weeks. They receive around €30-40 per day plus food and accommodation, usually in dormitories. The web site www.wwoof.org advertises short term job in farms permitting travellers to work in return for food and lodging.

There are also a considerable number of posts as guides, around France's many *châteaux*, other historical buildings and museums. Those speaking foreign languages are in particular demand. Applications should be sent directly to those responsible for each site. Their contact details can be obtained from local tourist offices (see a list of these, with telephone numbers etc, at www.tourisme.gouv.fr).

Au Pairs

In exchange for board and lodging with a family, and a modest allowance, *au pairs* look after children and also undertake varying degrees of housework. Some *au pairs* are treated very well, though many are expected to work very long hours and in some cases are subjected to rudeness and cruelty. The agencies that place *au pairs* often state that they have carried out checks on the families offering to take *au pairs*, and this does provide some protection, albeit somewhat limited. Agencies often arrange French language classes and other activities, which can reduce the feeling of isolation reported by many *au pairs*.

Ideally try to meet the family before you commit yourself. Your employer is responsible for informing the French social security authorities that they have taken you on and for making social security contributions on your behalf, to entitle you to health care under the French state health system.

For those who are poorly treated, the best advice is simply to leave, even if you have signed your name to a contract for several months. The chances of an employer taking legal action against you are very slight, and in any case, if you have been treated badly you will not only have a good defence, but you may have a claim against your employer. The best course of action is probably to ask the agency to find another post for you - *au pairs* are often in short supply. Ensure that you always have sufficient money, or access to money, to return home. If you are without funds, consider asking your parents or a friend to pay your airfare. Failing this, seek assistance from the nearest British consulate – they may be prepared to lend you the airfare (see Appendix 1 for the addresses of consulates).

Voluntary work

There are numerous possibilities for voluntary work, although you normally need to be over 16 (or sometimes 18) and generally under 30. The work, which is often on archaeological or conservation projects, is physically demanding. Though unpaid, board and lodging are provided (although this is normally very basic and often subject to a modest contribution by you). Participants remain responsible for their own travel costs, insurance and health cover. You should note that the common language is frequently English, and you need to be careful in your selection if you are hoping to have immersion in French.

Further guidance and advice

If you have any questions concerning access to jobs, employment rights or professional training the government runs a Service Info Emploi. Telephone enquiries are taken from 9.00 a.m. to 6.00 p.m. Monday to Friday on 825 347 347. The web site is at www.emploi-solidarite.gouv.fr. Alternative sources of advice on your rights include www.droitsdesjeunes.gouv.fr and www.legifrance.gouv.fr

General websites in English and some postal addresses

www.europa.eu.int/jobs/eures; www.webseurope.com; www.exposure-eu.com; www.eurojobs.com;

www.overseasjobs.com; www.escapeartist.com – a selection of jobs and also information and resources for living in France; www.justlanded .com – some jobs

Websites in French

www.anpe.fr; www.apec.fr; www.apec.asso.fr (for the employment of managers); www.cadresonline.com; www.rebondir.fr; www.go.tm.fr; www.jobpilot.net; www.emploiregions.com (said to have over 13,000 job offers on line), www.emploi.org, www.action-emploi.net, www.jobalacarte.com

Working on the Black Market

There are many foreigners and French working in France without making the appropriate declaration to the social security authorities. This is most common in the construction, farming and the various service industries, notably tourism. If discovered, employers face sentences of imprisonment up to two years and fines of up to €30,000. In theory an employee may also face a fine, though in some circumstances may be entitled to damages from the employer equivalent to up to six months salary. You should note that those employees working illegally have no rights to health cover or other benefits provided by the State.

Chapter Four

THE CONTRACT OF EMPLOYMENT, YOUR RIGHTS AND OBLIGATIONS

The contract of employment

This is an agreement between an employer and employee under which the employee agrees to carry out certain tasks in return for a wage or salary.

Contracts can be oral or in writing. It is obviously preferable to have a written contract, and most large companies do this. The contract should include the names of the parties, the start date, duration (if temporary), the workplace where the employee will work or be based, the employee's professional category or a job description, and the basic wage or salary and additional benefits. It should also record the number of ordinary work hours required per week and the times at which the employee will be required to work, holiday entitlement, and the period of notice required. Lastly the agreement should identify any collective agreement applicable to the employment relationship.

CDDs, and CDIs

Employers can offer either fixed-term contracts of up to nine months (*contrats à durée déterminée* or CDD) or more usually permanent contracts (*contrats à durée indéterminée* or CDI). Permanent contracts can be brought to an end, but only in accordance with the rules set out in the Labour Code. Fixed term contracts can only be offered for temporary employment, such as for the completion of a given task, for seasonal jobs, or for the temporary replacement of a permanent member of staff on maternity leave. A fixed term contract can be renewed once, giving a total duration of eighteen months. The contract must be in writing and state the purpose of the appointment, the remuneration, the start date and end date, the duration of any trial period. Failure to mention the reason why the contract is of limited duration will mean that the employment is deemed to be of indefinite duration thereby giving the employee full protection. Those on a fixed term contract are entitled to an end of contract bonus equivalent to 10% of the total gross salary paid. They are also entitled to compensation for paid holidays equivalent to 10% of gross salary and bonus. It is possible to have a trial period for a fixed term contract (i.e. a CDD), but it must not exceed two weeks for a contract lasting up to six months, and one month for a longer contract.

Agency contracts

Businesses are only able to use staff from temporary employment agencies for short-term tasks. The employee is employed by the temporary employment agency, though the business is not legally prevented from offering the person a direct permanent contract. Agency workers are entitled to the same end of contract bonuses as employees under a CDD (see the paragraph above). Contracts are limited to 18 months duration (including any renewal).

Training contracts

Le contrat de professionnalisation has now replaced the former *contrat de qualification, d'orientation et d'adaptation*. It is designed for those who are unemployed and aged 26 and over, and also for those aged 16-25 who have completed a course of training or further education. The employer must offer either a permanent contract of employment, or a fixed term contract of six to twelve months, and must provide the employee with training courses that cover a total of 15-25% of the employee's hours under the contract. The contract can be renewed once, though it can also be renewed should the employee fail a test or examination, or be unable to work due to illness or accident. The employer is not required to fund the employee's training, which for those previously unemployed is met by ASSEDIC.

Those under 21 receive 55% of the SMIC (the minimum wage), increased to 65% if they have a *bac professionnel* or similar qualification. Those between 21 and 25 receive 70% and 80% respectively of the SMIC. Employers receive substantial relief in respect of social security contributions in relation to those under 26, and those aged 45 and over and previously unemployed.

Le contrat nouvelles embauches (CNE)

A new form of contract, introduced in 2005, it is designed to encourage small businesses to take on staff by providing them with greater freedom to reduce staffing levels should they need to do so. This is a contract of indefinite duration, a type of CDI, designed for small business undertakings with a maximum of 20 employees. It must be in writing. It is subject to all the usual rules governing CDIs, save that if the business encounters difficulties during the first two years of the contract, an employer can quickly terminate the employment contract by notifying the employee by registered letter with *avis de réception*. The employer does not have to give any reason for bringing the contract to an end. The notice period is two weeks from the end of the first month to the end of the sixth month of employment, rising thereafter to one month's notice. The notice period starts from the date that the letter is received by the employee. The employer must also make a payment to the employee to cover holidays that have not yet been taken, and a payment of 8% of the total gross salary received by the employee during the contract. This latter payment is tax-free and is not subject to any social security contributions. If the business picks up, then an employer can enter into a new *contrat nouvelles embauches*, even with the same employee, providing three months have passed since the termination of the previous contract. Once an employee is employed for two years, then his contract of employment automatically becomes a standard CDI.

Le contrat Jeunes en Entreprise

This is reserved for those aged 16 to 22 with no or only limited qualifications. The contract of employment must be a permanent contract, and can be full or part-time, provided the employee works at least 50% of the hours of a full-time employee. The employer receives up to €300 per month during the first two years of the contract, reduced by 50% for the third year. The employee must be paid at least the national minimum wage, or the minimum wage fixed by any collective labour agreement.

Le Contrat Initiative Emploi (CEI)

This is designed to assist the long-term unemployed over 25, or those with dependent children, to return to the workplace. The applicant must have been unemployed for at least 18 out of the previous 36 months, or 12 out of the last 18 for those living in urban areas. The contract can be either permanent or for a fixed term of from one to two years, and must be for at least 20 hours per week. The employer receives a substantial subsidy which is fixed by the *préfet* in each region, but which cannot exceed 47% of the SMIC. Depending upon his financial circumstances the employee may also be able to continue to receive some unemployment benefit.

Le Contrat Insertion (RMI)

This is reserved for those who have been in receipt of supplementary benefit (RMI), or certain other benefits for at least six months and who are having difficulty entering or re-entering the job market. The contract of employment must be for at least six months during which the employer receives a subsidy equal to the supplementary benefit payable to a single person.

Seasonal work contracts

These are CDDs that must not exceed 8 months. They are designed for sectors of the economy that experience seasonal variations in demand for labour, in particular agriculture and tourism. They must be in writing, and state the reason that they have been entered into. With a seasonal contract, there is no "bonus" paid at the end of the contract as with a standard CDI (see above).

Part-time contracts

These must be in writing. Employees will need to work at least 60 hours per month to receive social security coverage.

Le chèque emploi service

This system applies to domestic employees, gardeners or those who look after or educate children in their employer's homes, but who work for not more than 8 hours per week. An employee can work for several such employers, providing he does not exceed 40 hours per week. The cheque replaces the contract of employment, the pay slip and the request for registration with the social security system. An employer obtains a "cheque book" from his bank or a post-office, completes a form and sends it with his bank details to the Centre National de Traitement de Chèque Emploi Service Social (CNICES). Security contributions for the employee are deducted from an employer's bank account by the CNICES. The employer completes the cheques to pay the employee, each time sending a notification to CNICES, which then sends a pay slip to the employee. The advantage of the system for the employer is that he receives a reduction in his personal tax bill equal to 50% of the amount paid to the employee. In some circumstances the employer can also obtain an exemption in relation to social charges.

Remuneration

This is provided for in the contract of employment, but may also be the subject of collective bargaining. In addition to a basic salary workers often have fringe benefits related to length of service or consisting of bonuses, profit-sharing, distance and transport bonuses, workplace bonuses for difficulty of work, or unsocial hours, or dangers involved or for quality or quantity of production.

Le salaire brut is the salary paid by the employer, whereas *le salaire net* is after deduction of social contributions of 20-25%. French law provides for a minimum wage. This is currently just over €1,150 per month (*brut*) for a 35 hour week, with an hourly rate of €7.61. The minimum wage is increased by 25% for those in semi-skilled employment, and by 50% for skilled workers. Employees generally receive a13th month salary payment by way of an annual bonus.

Working time

The concept of the 35 hour week introduced by the previous socialist administration has been retained, though there is now much more flexibility. Employees can now be obliged to work up to 220 additional hours (*heures supplémentaires*) per year, and have the right to work further additional hours by agreement. Overtime must be paid at a rate not less than 10% above the standard hourly rate. If there is no collective agreement between employer and employees then overtime must be paid at time and a quarter for the first eight hours of overtime, and thereafter at time and a half.

Employees are not normally permitted to work for more than 10 hours per day, nor more than six days per week.

Holidays

The usual holiday entitlement is five weeks a year, or two and a half days of paid leave per four-week period worked. Employees may have to wait until they have been employed twelve months before they are permitted to take this leave. In addition there are eleven public holidays (seen the Appendices). The majority of the French still take much of their holiday entitlement during August. A husband and wife (or partners to a PACS) who work in the same undertaking are entitled to take their holidays together. Employees have an additional right to an extra day's holiday if they take 3-5 of their days of holiday entitlement outside the usual holiday period of 1st May to 31st October, and two days if they take six or more days outside this period.

Sickness leave

If your doctor considers that you are unable to work he will complete a form Cerfa No 10170*02. You must complete a section of the form and send the form within 48 hours to the social security scheme and to your employer. You are not permitted to work whilst receiving sickness benefit.

Maternity and paternity leave

Expectant mothers are entitled to at least six weeks' leave prior to the estimated delivery date, and a further ten weeks after. If you have already given birth to at least two children, and have at least two dependent children you are entitled to twenty-six weeks (eight before the birth and eighteen afterwards). An expectant mother will have seven routine ante-natal appointments and is entitled to take these during work hours without any deduction of salary or other sanction by her employer.

All fathers who are employees or participating in a vocational training scheme, are entitled to paternity pay, as are some categories of the self-employed. It consists of eleven consecutive days leave for the case of a single birth, and eighteen days for multiple births, and is in addition to the three days leave granted on the birth of an employee's child. The leave can be taken at any time within four months of the date of the birth, but cannot be split. The leave can be postponed where the baby is hospitalised, or the mother has died. Employees are required to give employers one month's notice of their return to work. Paternity leave allowance is paid by the social security authorities.

Training

Those in employment are entitled to undertake part-time or full time training course of their choice. A full-time course can be up to one year, or possibly longer (contact FONGECIF for further information). They receive up to 100% of their salary, and can obtain payment of training expenses. The course does not have to relate to their present occupation, or to the employer's undertaking, and can be taken with a view to a career change, or to gain cultural or social skills. The employment contract is not terminated, but merely suspended.

End of the contract of employment

This can come about by mutual agreement, or according to the terms originally agreed in the contract, or because of the expiry of a fixed term contact, or due to resignation, death, serious invalidity or retirement. It can also arise as a result of natural disasters, redundancy, dismissal, or constructive dismissal (where an employee justifiably leaves his employment in response to unacceptable conduct on the part of the employer). If you simply wish to end your employment, where there is no fault on the part of your employer then you should give your employer the notice provided in your employment contract.

Redundancy

If an employer wishes to make an employee redundant on economic grounds or because of a material change in his business, he must adopt the procedure prescribed by law. The employer must take all steps to train and adapt employees, and investigate possibilities of re-employment in the same or equivalent job category, or failing which, in a lower employment category if the employee consents to this. Where there are large-scale redundancies and there are employee representatives, the employer has to put his case for a redundancy to the employment authorities by presenting a restructuring plan, and the employees must be given the opportunity to respond to the employer's case for dismissal.

The employees may only be dismissed if the plan is approved by the employment authorities. At least one UK company has found itself in difficulties by failing to follow the correct procedures in relation to its French staff.

Dismissal

An employer is entitled to discipline employees for misconduct including physical or verbal abuse, fighting, theft, disobedience, drunkenness, breach of confidence. Disciplinary action can include written and verbal warnings, and dismissal in the case of continued breaches or a single serious breach. An employer is not permitted to dismiss an employee because of his ethnic origin, religion, sex or sexual orientation, political opinions, membership of a trade union, pregnancy, or for exercising a right, such as making a complaint. An employer may only dismiss on health or disability grounds if the correct procedures are adopted, including the obtaining of an appropriate medical opinion.

Prior to dismissal the employer must invite the employee to an interview by registered letter. If the reason for a proposed dismissal is disciplinary in nature, the employer must make the invitation not later than two months after discovering the offence. If the undertaking has no employee representative, then the letter must give the employee at least five days prior to the interview in order for him to take advice, and to have the opportunity to find someone to attend the interview with him, such as a work colleague, or an adviser. At the interview the employer must explain the reason for the proposed dismissal and listen to the employee's explanation. If the employer decides on dismissal, notification must be sent to the employee by registered letter, stating the precise reason for the dismissal. The employee then has a right of an appeal to an employment tribunal, called *Le Conseil des Prud'hommes*.

If the tribunal finds in favour of the employee, and the employee has been employed by the employer for more than two years, and the employer has more than eleven employees, then the tribunal can order that the employee be reinstated. If the employer then fails to re-employ the person, it is liable to pay compensation of at least six month's salary. Employees with less than two years' employment can still bring a claim for unfair dismissal, but have no right to reinstatement and can only be awarded damages for the earnings that they have in fact lost.

"Forced" resignations, and resignations "in the heat of the moment".

If an employee resigns in response to unreasonable conduct on the part of the employer, he or she should state this in his letter notifying the employer of his decision to resign. In such circumstances, leaving can amount to a "constructive dismissal", giving an employee the right to bring a claim before the tribunal for unfair dismissal. You would be wise to take immediate legal advice before deciding to resign.

If you resign on the spur of the moment, whether orally or in writing, in anger, despair or irritation then your employer may be legally bound to allow you to change your mind. If you do wish to retract a resignation, do so as soon as possible, and in writing.

Restrictions imposed on employees

Employees must not use information that they learn during their employment, such as trade secrets and lists of clients, but owe a duty of confidentiality to their employer. Employers often try to extend this protection by including clauses in the contract of employment that seek to forbid or restrict the employee from working for competing companies after they have left. In French law these *clauses de non-concurrence* are only enforceable if they are limited to two years, limited geographically and limited to a specific kind of work. In addition the employee must be given compensation amounting to up to a two-thirds increase in his salary level. If you are considering branching out on your own, or moving to another employer and suspect that you may be in breach of such a clause, you should take legal advice as to its enforceability.

The employment of women

There is a prohibition on employing women in certain dangerous and polluting employments. Women must not carry, pull or push weights over 25 kg. Women who are pregnant, and whose normal work involves contact with chemicals or certain products, must be offered a temporary change of work. Pregnant women receive maternity benefit from the CPAM and an additional allowance from the employer, up until one month after their return from maternity leave.

Employers are not permitted to require pregnant women to work for more than ten hours per day, to undertake difficult tasks, or to work for two weeks prior to the expected delivery date, and during the six weeks after the birth.

Pregnant woman who work between 21.00 and 06.00 hours (night work) are entitled to a temporary change to a day job. If this is not possible, the employment contract is suspended during which the woman receives guaranteed pay consisting of a daily allowance paid by the CPAM and an additional allowance paid by the employer.

Workers under 18

The legal minimum working age is 16. Children aged 14 and over can work during school holidays, providing they do not work for more than half the vacation, and the holidays last for at least 14 days. They must not work for more than four and a half hours at a time, during which there must be a break of at least 30 minutes. Night work (i.e. from 20.00 to 06.00) is not permitted. Children under 16 are not permitted to carry out repetitive tasks, must first be seen by a *médecin du travail* and need their parents written consent to work. Employers must also ask for permission from the *inspection du travail* at least 15 days prior to the start of a work contract. In practice employers find these requirements too demanding, and generally prefer to employ those over 18. The under-16s must receive remuneration of at least 80% of the SMIC.

Those between 16 and 18 need their parents' written consent to work, but the employer is no longer required to obtain the consent of the *inspection du travail*. They must not work for more than 35 hours in a week, or more than 7 hours in a day, and cannot work between 22.00 and 06.00. They cannot be obliged to work on Sundays or public holidays, save in the hotel and restaurant sectors or in hospitals. Under-18s may not be employed to carry out dangerous work, and may not work in bars. They must be paid at least 90% of the SMIC.

The earnings of those under 18 form part of the parents' income for tax purposes, and must be included on their tax return.

A minor must be given a written contract by his employer, however short the period of employment. It must specify the work to be carried out, the place of work and the duration of the contract.

Protection against sexual harassment

If you believe that you have been subject to harassment on the grounds of your sex you have a right to bring a complaint. Sexual harassment consists of the kind of behaviour that is aimed at obtaining sexual favours for the perpetrator or for another person. All employees are protected, as are job candidates and those on training courses. An employer must not penalise any employee who has suffered or refused to put up with sexual harassment, or who witnesses or reports such conduct. Any employee who considers that he has been prejudiced in any way, for example by a failure to be promoted, can bring a claim before an employment tribunal. The victim can request that any court proceedings be brought by his or her trade union on his or her behalf. Once a complainant has established the facts that suggest sexual harassment, it is then for the accused to prove that there was no sexual harassment, and that the conduct is explained by other reasons. Employees found guilty of sexual harassment must be subject to disciplinary action. Such conduct is also a criminal offence carrying a sentence of one-year imprisonment and a fine of €15,000.

Discrimination

French law prohibits sexual and racial discrimination, and also discrimination on the grounds of age, marital status, language, religious and political beliefs, trade union membership and disability.

Employee representation

The task of employee representatives is to represent other employees both individually and collectively across the whole range of issues relating to employment. He or she is also required to inform the authorities of complaints by staff and failure to comply with safety regulations. Representatives can be called upon to accompany employees at disciplinary interviews. They must be informed and consulted before redundancies are made. In smaller undertakings with less than 50 employees, employee representatives are consulted about periods of paid leave, organisation of working time, training issues, and redeployment of injured employees.

Trade Unions

Where there is a trade union, employees' interests are represented by shop stewards, who perform similar duties to those set out in the paragraph above. They are entitled to between 10 and 20 hours a month to carry out their task, depending upon the size of the undertaking for which they work.

Work disputes

Employment disputes are generally brought before the *Conseil des Prud'hommes*. These courts are akin to the UK's Employment Tribunals, with cases being heard by tribunals made up of representatives of employees and employers.

Employees have the right to strike, but to be within the law a strike must comply with specific legal regulations. A strike must involve the total cessation of work by those on strike, must be collective, must be of only short duration, and be for a purpose connected with the strikers' employment. It is illegal to carry out a "go-slow" involving deliberately slowing down the pace of work, to undertake a "work to rule" or to take part in a political strike. Employers are permitted to make deductions from employees' salaries relating to the time not worked, but may not discriminate against strikers in relation to pay or social benefits. Employers are required to continue to pay non-strikers unless they can prove that it was not possible to give them work.

Strikers are required to respect the rights of non-strikers. Preventing others from working is an offence that can result in dismissal. Employers and non-strikers are entitled to bring claims for damages, against trade unions and those on strike, for losses suffered from illegal conduct during a strike.

Further guidance and advice

If you have any questions concerning access to jobs, employment rights or professional training the government runs a Service Info Emploi. Telephone enquiries are taken from 09.00 to 18.00 Monday to Friday on 0825 347 347. The web site is at: www.emploi-solidarite.gouv.fr. Further information on employees' rights and obligations can be found at www.travail.gouv.fr

Chapter Five

INCOME TAX AND SOCIAL SECURITY CONTRIBUTIONS

French rules on residency for the purposes of income tax

In brief French law deems you to be a resident in France for income tax purposes if:

- France is your main residence or home; or
- France is the place that you spend most of your time, generally 183 days, but less could be sufficient, where for example the rest of the year is divided between other countries and the greatest number of days are spent in France; or
- Your principal occupation or business is in France, or main income arises in France; or
- Your most substantial assets are in France

It is possible for one married partner to be resident in the UK for tax purposes, and the other to be resident in France. France has double taxation agreements with most other European countries. Information on the agreement with the UK is available on www.inlandrevenue.gov.uk

Taxation and social security in practice for those in employment

Employed by a UK employer, but living in France

Those who are sent by their UK employer to live and work in France temporarily as part of their job will normally remain subject to the UK system of taxation and national insurance. Their tax and national insurance contributions should be deducted at source by their UK employer. In theory they remain liable to pay French income tax, and should submit an annual income tax declaration in March. Credit is given for the UK tax paid. As French income tax is lower than that in the UK in practice no additional income tax is generally payable. As far a social security is concerned, they receive a form E101. This entitles them to the same health cover under the French system as a French citizen. This means that they obtain reimbursement from the French authorities (see the chapter entitled *Healthcare and the French Health System*). The French authorities will then recover this from the UK authorities. Not all medical costs are covered in full – in particular post-operative outpatient care, and you should consider taking out a *mutuelle* to cover the balance. Your employer will need to apply for a fresh E101 each year. The French authorities are reluctant to grant more than one extension (i.e. cover for a total of two years), though they can and do grant annual extensions giving cover of up to five years. They consider that after that, the employee is in reality permanently based in France and should be covered under the French system. E101 cover is also available for the self-employed who are working in France temporarily.

Employed in the UK, with your family living in France

Where a person is living and working in the UK, an E109 will be issued to cover the person's dependants in France. If, however, you are resident in France, the relevant form is an E106 that covers both your dependants and you for health cover in France. Accordingly if the worker is in practice returning to stay with his family in France at weekends and holidays then the appropriate form is an E106, whereas if he only returns every few months then an E109 would clearly be the correct form. Both national insurance and UK income tax will be deducted by the UK employer. If the person is resident in France then he should submit an annual income tax declaration in March. The UK tax paid is taken into account, and in practice no additional income tax is usually payable.

Living and working in France for a French based employer

As to social security contributions, the greater part of an employee's contributions is paid by the employer. An employee's contribution can still be significant i.e. up to 13.6% of gross salary. Contributions are deductible against income tax. The system of income tax is based on what is termed *le quotient familial*. The taxable income of each household is divided into a number of parts that depends on marital status and the number of children or other dependants. In brief, a couple with several dependent children pay significantly less tax than those with no dependants. Unmarried partners who have registered a PACS can make a joint declaration as for married couples, and no longer have to wait for three years. Those unmarried and living together, and who have not registered a PACS must make separate tax returns. In practice around half of French adults pay no income tax at all.

Self-employed with a business in France

Details of the tax rules for the self-employed and those in business are included in Chapter 6.

Chapter Six

SETTING UP AND RUNNING A
BUSINESS IN FRANCE

Starting a business in any country requires a considerable degree of planning, in particular realistic sales forecasts, and estimates of start up costs and cash flow. In France, despite recent increases, the rate of new business creations is still one of the lowest in Europe, and less than half the rate in the UK. Experts attribute this discrepancy to unwillingness of the French to take risks, but important factors are the heavy burden paid by businesses in social security payments, and the considerable bureaucracy faced by new businesses.

UK citizens intending to start a business in France have added difficulties arising from the fact that are operating wholly or partly in a foreign language and also in a system with which they are unfamiliar. Inevitably these factors significantly increase the amount of time that they have to put into the business, as well as some of their starting and running costs, which are only partly reduced if the business is primarily catering for other English-speakers. Whatever type of business you intend to run, you must be able to speak French to a reasonable level or select a business adviser who is fluent in both French and English, as well as experienced in advising businesses in France.

Obtaining advice and assistance

Good starting points for advice and assistance in English are the French Embassy, which has a number of leaflets and booklets available in English (see www.ambafrance.org.uk), the French chamber of commerce in the UK (www.ccfgb.co.uk), and the Franco-British and American Chambers of Commerce in France (www.francobritishchambers.com, www.bccriviera.com and www.amchamfrance.org). The chambers of commerce often hold seminars, conferences, discussions and workshops. They are not only invaluable sources of information, but also useful means of establishing contacts with fellow English speakers running a business in France, and who have already encountered many of the difficulties that face newcomers. Information in English on establishing a business in France is also available from UK Trade and Investment, Kingsgate House, 66-74 Victoria Street, London SW1E 6SW Tel 020 7 215 5000 (web site:

www.uktradeinvest.gov.uk).

You will definitely need a competent chartered accountant and/or commercial lawyer to advise on the structure of your business (see below). He can also provide you with up-to-date advice on financial support available to businesses, such as subsidies, grants and tax incentives, draft a standard contract for your business, and assist you with the formalities of creating a business. If you are unemployed, the DDTEFP (*Direction Départementale du Travail, de l'Emploi et de la Formation Professionnelle*) can provide vouchers that enable you to obtain advice from an *avocat, notaire* or *expert-comptable* at only €15.24 an hour, with the balance of €45.74 being paid by the government.

A useful montly publication is *L'Entreprise* (see also its web site www.lentreprise.com). The book *Création de sociétés innovantes: guide pratique* by Lison Chouraki can be downloaded without charge on the web site www.groupconstantin.com. Information can also be obtained from the portals www.minefi.gouv.fr www.entreprises.minefi.gouv.fr

Government agencies that can help you

There is a host of government bodies that provide advice and assistance, in some cases financial. The ANPE (*l'Agence Nationale Pour l'Emploi*) organises interviews and workshops to help those wishing to start up their own business, as well as free courses in French for foreigners. It is well worth calling in to your nearest branch, as well as consulting their web site www.anpe.fr. Another invaluable source of information consulted by many people starting their own business is the local *Chambre de Commerce et d'Industrie* (CCI) which will have specialist advisers. In some areas courses are held in English. Other agencies offering advice include:

- APEC (*L'Association Pour l'Emploi des Cadres*), which also holds workshops (www.apec.fr)
- ASSEDIC – visit the Demandeurs d'emploi section of the site www.assedic.fr and chose "*Situations et professions particulières*").
- APCE (*L'Agence Pour la Création d'Entreprise*) www.apce.com (see under *Créer Une Entreprise*)
- ADIE (*L'Association pour le développement de l'initiative économique*) grants loans to those who cannot obtain bank finance and provides advice (www.adie.org).
- FranceActive: this body guarantees bank loans and gives financial support and advice to the unemployed seeking to create a new business (www.franceactive.org).

- Réseau + assists those wishing to create a new business in the service industries (www.reseau-plus.net)
- La Boutique de Gestion – an independent but state-sponsored network of over 200 branches helping with the setting up of new businesses (web site: www.boutiques-de-gestion.com).

The recognition of your UK qualifications

A wide range of occupations is subject to specific restrictions and regulations. You must make enquiries of the relevant professional body. In the past foreigners have found it difficult to have their qualifications recognized, and to establish themselves in France. In recent years, however, as officialdom has been obliged to adapt its rules to comply with European regulations, foreigners have found that the situation has improved considerably. For further details on the recognition of qualifications see the section Having your qualifications recognised in Chapter 3. Those who are self-employed and want to have their experience recognised should contact the Department of Trade and Industry and ask for a guidance pack about having your experience recognised (Certificate of Experience Unit, DTI European Policy Directorate, Bay 211/212 Kingsgate House, 66-74 Victoria Street, London SW1E 6SW tel: 0207 215 4648).

Choosing the business structure

There is a far greater range of different business structures in France, than in the UK. Those listed below are the most popular, particularly amongst British ex-patriots.

L'Entreprise individuelle (EI)

This is favoured by those who wish to work on their own, and is the structure adopted by most of the British who are operating businesses in France. No minimum capital is required, it costs only €59.19 to set up and nothing to run. You are required to register the business within two weeks of starting (see below).

The disadvantage of an *enterprise individuelle* is that you are personally liable for all business debts, and accordingly you could be compelled to sell private assets should the business fail. Under a new provision introduced in 2004 you can now protect your home from creditors. This is done by making a *déclaration d'insaisissabilité* (declaration on non-seizability) before a *notaire*. This *must* be then registered with the *Bureau des Hypothèques* and published in the local official newspaper. Married couples are jointly responsible for each other's debts, and when going into business you should consider opting for *la séparation de biens* to protect your spouse's assets (see the discussion of this in Chapter 8).

A person operating as an *enterprise universelle* is, of course, obliged to charge TVA and to account to the authorities for this. The profit or loss from the business is added to any other income for income tax purposes. In addition you will be required to pay the *taxe professionnelle*.

La Société à Responsabilité Limitée (SARL)

This is a limited liability company with from 2 to 30 shareholders, and is often chosen by British residents in France. There is no mimium share capital. Shareholders' liability in the event of the company failing is limited to the value of their shareholding, although your liability will obviously be greater if you personally guarantee the company's bank account. The company will need to appoint a managing director, and select a registered office (*siège social*). This can be at rented business premises, your home address (if you are a tenant, you do not need the landlord's consent for the first two years), or simply a letterbox company address with a *société de domiciliation*.

L'Entreprise Unipersonelle à Responsabilité Limitée (EURL).

This is similar to the SARL, save that there is only one shareholder. This will not be apparent from your business stationery. The share capital required is now only one euro, though you may wish to invest more, as the amount will be stated on your letterhead. You will need to select a registered office (*siège social*), as for a SARL (see above).

La Société Anonyme

This is akin to a plc in the UK, and requires a minimum share capital of €37,000.

La société par actions simplifiée

This relatively new structure is thought to be more flexible than either the SA or SARL. It permits entrepreneurs to search for investors in the company, without losing control of their business. As with an SA, liability is limited to the share capital introduced, though this must be at least €37,000. Only half of this has to be provided at start-up, with the rest being introduced over a period of up to five years.

La société civile immobilière (SCI)

This is a company formed for the purposes of buying, selling and managing property, and is often used by landlords as a means of holding property. Ownership in the property can be effectively passed on by selling or gifting shares in the company, rather than transferring the property itself which remains in the company name. This can have tax advantages. An SCI is not permitted to trade. Those resident for tax purposes in the UK should be wary of using an SCI to hold property if they intend to occupy it themselves, for example for holidays. The UK tax authorities may determine that their occupation is payment in kind to them by the company, for which they can be assessed for income tax.

Working with your spouse

There are three different forms in which one spouse can assist in the business of his or her partner: as *conjoint collaborateur* (if you operate as an *entreprise individuelle*, or as a single owner of a EURL), *conjoint associé* (if you operate as a company and your spouse is a shareholder) and *conjoint salarié* (where your spouse is your employee, or an employee of your company). As a *conjoint collaborateur*, the spouse works without being paid, but receives health cover and maternity benefits. After ten years the un-paid spouse becomes entitled to a capital sum on the eventual death of his or her partner (which is not subject to inheritance tax), and in some circumstances can be entitled to his or her partner's pension rights on the partner's death. If you are going to receive assistance from your partner in the running of a business, you need to discuss the possible options with an accountant or lawyer.

Your business name

Note, that whichever structure you opt for, you should check with the *Institut National de la Propriété Industrielle* that the name that you intend to use for your business is not already in use (see www.impi.fr, or telephone 08 36 293630).

Registering your business

You should do this by paying a visit to the local *Centre de formalités des entreprises* (CFE) that will pass on the relevant details to all the necessary government bodies. There are different types of CFE depending upon your activity. Retailers, shopkeepers and others in the service industry register with the *Chambre de commerce et d'industrie*, those in the building trade with the *Chambre des métiers* and those in the liberal professions (surveyors, doctors, dentists, lawyers, accountants) with the URSSAF. For details of the addresses and contact details of all CFEs see www.sirene.tm.fr/annuaire.cfe

The CFE will advise you on the documentation required, including documentation specifically relevant to your business activity. The papers required will include a certificate showing that you have a clean criminal record (this is obtained from the *Casier Judiciaire National* and can be obtained on-line from www.justice.gouv.fr/cjn/demb3.htm). You will also need the title deeds or lease of the premises from which you intend to operate. You must give details of the name under which you wish to operate – for the liberal professions this must be your own name.

When you have registered your business with the relevant CFE you will be given a *Récépissé de Création d'Entreprise*. This will include your SIREN or business number. You may not start operating, however, until you receive your K-bis, which is an extract of your entry on the *Registre du Commerce et des Sociétés* or *Répertoire des Métiers* (for artisans). Shortly thereafter you should receive your full business number or SIRET, which consists of the SIREN that you have already received, together with some further digits. The SIRET must appear on all your business stationery, including invoices, estimates and receipts.

Business premises

The procedure for the purchase of business premises is very similar to that for purchasing residential premises (see *The Complete Guide to Buying Property in France*, written by this author and published by Kogan Page). A large proportion of business premises are leased. French law gives a certain amount of protection to the business tenant, most importantly a right to the renewal of the lease. It is essential, however, that you bear in mind the exceptions to this right, and comply with the regulations governing the renewal of the lease. It is imperative to take advice from a lawyer. The tenant has a right to compensation where the landlord establishes that he is entitled to refuse a renewal (unless the tenant has breached the terms of the lease). Business leases generally contain a restriction on the nature of the business activity that may be carried on from the premises.

Finding a business and/or premises to purchase

A business is termed a *fonds de commerce*, and is distinct from *les murs* or *les locaux* which are the business premises. There are several different ways of searching for a business to purchase, with or without premises. Many of the estate agents, British and French, that handle residential premises, also deal with the sale of businesses. You will also see them advertised in the various English-language French property magazines and French property web sites. *French Property News* (www.french-property-news.com) and *French News* (www.french-news.com) are two potential starting places. The French national weekly *ICF L'Argus de Commerce* is worth taking a look at, although once you know the region in which you want to purchase a business, you should also search the local newspapers.

Once you have located a business to purchase, you should insist upon working in the business for a while before you enter into any agreement to purchase. This will enable you to assess the accuracy of the turnover figures that you have been given, and learn more about the running of the business prior to committing yourself.

Even if you are not purchasing the business property, you should consult a lawyer to represent you in relation to your purchase of a business. Ensure that he has a full understanding of your business plan.

Permits and licences

Changes to a shop-front or to a business sign do not normally require any form of permission, though you will need to lodge a *déclaration de travaux exempts de permis de construire* with the *Mairie*. You will also need to apply for a *permis* for a change of use, or an increase in size of more than 20 metres squared. Any new business opening in shop premises in excess of 300 metres squared must have authorisation from the *préfecture*. "Bed and Breakfast" premises must register with the local *Mairie* and *Préfecture* though if there are more than five bedrooms a more complex registration procedure applies.

Business franchises

For those considering starting a franchise business you should take a look at www.ac-franchise.com, www.franchise-fff.com (the site of *La Fédération Française de la Franchise*) and www.observatoiredelafranchise.com. At the time of writing www.angloinfo.com was seeking franchisees for different regions of France.

Working from home

Well over half of new businesses are started from home. Under recent legislation this has now become easier for those living in rented accommodation – they can now register their business at their home address for up to five years without their landlord's consent, providing they do not receive customers or deliveries of goods to their home, and are working from their principal residence. Those living in a *copropriété*, however, will still need to check that there are no regulations governing the block or the development that prevent them from running a business.

Those working from home benefit from additional tax allowances. You can set off one third of expenses such as heating against your business income. If you are in business under your own name, and own your home this can now be protected from your creditors (see under *L'Entreprise individuelle*, above).

Obtaining finance

Whether you are approaching a government organisation, or a private bank, you will need a detailed business plan to support your application. This must include an assessment of the demand for your product or service, the likely income, the capital or other assets that you are going to introduce into the business, and the fixed and variable costs. You will also need to produce some cash flow forecasts to show how your business will survive the first three years.

State aid and other assistance

There are various subsidised loans, grants and subsidies available from the European Union, central, regional and local government, particularly in the less prosperous regions. A useful starting point is www.subsidies-in-france.com where you can find assistance for identifying and applying for a host of different forms of financial assistance. There are also various loan guarantee schemes in which state organisations provide a guarantee to your bank for the repayment of a loan.

Other organisations worth contacting are your local *Mairie*, your local *Chambre de Commerce*, DATAR (www.datar.gouv.fr), *France Initiative Réseau* (www.fir.asso.fr) and *Banque de Développement des Petites et Moyennes Entreprises* (www.bdpme.fr). The latter offers a variety of different loans, both for the creation and expansion of businesses.

The loans are generally dependent upon the borrower raising a similar sum independently, and are up to €76,000, though they can be higher if you are purchasing a business.

There is an additional source of loans and loan guarantees available for women wishing to start a business, distributed by the *Fonds de Garantie à l'Initiative des Femmes* (see the web site www.droits-femmes.gouv.fr).

If you wish to open a *gîte* and need carry out work to the property, there is substantial finance available in the form of grants from *Gîtes de France*. There are conditions attached to such grants, but they are well worth investigating.

Those in search of employment who wish to set up their own business are entitled to a range of different forms of assistance including tax reductions and rebates, subsidies and loans. Many benefit from l'Accre (*Aide aux Chômeurs Créateurs ou Repreneurs d'Entreprise*) which provides exemption from social charges for twelve months.

Those over 50 can benefit from assistance provided by Eden (*Encouragement au développement des entrepriese nouvelles*) in the form of an interest-free loan up to €6,098 repayable over five years. You should take advice in particular on the timing of the start of your business – you may increase your entitlement to state benefits by holding back the start date until your plans are more fully finalised.

The government has created 41 "*zones franches*" or development zones across France. Companies relocating to these disadvantaged areas that include a number of rural areas, are exempt from corporation tax, income tax and several other taxes for a period of five years, though at least one third of their workforce must be from the locality. For further details see the web site www.travail.gouv.fr/fse.

In addition, there are several tax incentives and allowances in the early years of a business. Certain types of new business fall within the category *Jeune Entreprise Innovante (JEI)* and can claim tax relief for up to eight years (see www.impots.gouv.fr and look for JEI).

Bank Finance

French banks tend to be more reluctant to grant business loans than their UK equivalents. They are unlikely to lend more than 70% of the cost of a business purchase, or the purchase of business premises. You are best advised to call upon the assistance of an accountant or business lawyer before approaching a bank, and to investigate the possibilities of obtaining other financial assistance first, including loan guarantees.

Insurance

It is a legal requirement to have insurance for employees and property, as well as for any vehicles owned or operated by the business. You should note that the notification period for claims is generally very short.

Taxation of business revenue

When deciding on investing in the business by purchasing substantial assets, such as a computer system, you should note that not all the costs are deductible against tax in the year in which they are purchased. The cost of such assets will be spread over a number of years and only a proportion will be deductible against tax in the year of purchase. You may wish to consider leasing equipment where tax deductions are more in line with your expenditure. You should, of course, keep records of your various expenses, in order to have these deducted against the business's revenue. It is vital to instruct a competent accountant (*expert-comptable*) to advise you in relation to your tax affairs.

Those running a business pay either *impôts sur le revenu* (income tax) or *impôts sur les sociétés* (corporation tax), depending on which form of structure is adopted. Those operating as an *Entreprise Individuelle* pay *impôts sur le revenu*, whilst those operating an *EURL* (i.e. a one-shareholder company) can chose which tax to pay, and generally opt to pay *impôts sur le revenu* (apart from anything else, it is easy to change from paying income tax to paying corporation tax, and not possible to change in the opposite direction).

A *SARL* pays corporation tax, except for a *SARL de famille*, and the salary of a minority director, which are subject to income tax.

Those paying *impôts sur le revenu* can also choose between three different types of tax regimes : *micro-entreprises, régime simplifié* and *régime réel*.

Under the Micro regime you deduct a fixed amount from your turnover to cover your expenses in order to arrive at your gross income for tax and social security purposes, and can use a simplified bookkeeping procedure with no obligation to present a full set of annual accounts. In most cases this results in substantially lower tax and social security bills than if you opt for the *régime réel* in which you deduct only the expenditure actually incurrred. The micro system is only available to the *entreprise individuelle* or *EURL* paying income tax and with a limited turnover (€27,000 for commercial services, and €76,300 for those selling goods), and who are not registered for VAT.

Where your turnover exceeds the micro thresholds you are taxed according to the *régime simplifié*. Here you make annual VAT declarations, and pay estimates of your VAT liability every three months with the balance paid (or refunded) at the end of each year. You deduct your actual expenses in order to arrive at your gross income for tax and social security purposes. You can opt instead for the *régime réel*. If your turnover exceeds €763,000 for commercial business and €230,000 for services, you must in any event change to the latter system. The main difference between these two relates to the payment of VAT – for the *régime réel* you must make monthly payments and declarations, inevitably placing a larger paperwork burden on your business.

Value Added Tax (VAT or TVA)

The system of value added tax (*taxe sur la valeur ajoutée*) is similar to that in the UK – businesses charge VAT to clients, and periodically pay this to the *Centre des Impôts* after deducting VAT that they have paid on their input. Small business are exempt (see above). The standard rate is 19.6%, with only 5.5% applying to certain items, such as hotel accommodation and books.

Other taxes on business

There are a number of other taxes on business activity, notably:

- *taxe sur les salaires*:
  this is a tax paid by businesses that are exempt or partially exempt from VAT (TVA), and ranges from 4.25% to 9.35% of the total payroll bill, less certain reductions;

- *taxe d'apprentissage*:
  this tax is payable by all business (save for the liberal professions and small

businesses employing trainees). It is levied on the gross
value of employees' salaries, at a rate of 0.5%;

* *la participation à la formation professionnelle continue*:
  this is a tax to finance professional training. The rate varies from
  between 0.1% and 0.15% of the gross salary bill, although this is
  reduced if you are incurring costs in training your own employees

* *participation à l'effort de construction*;
  this is a tax to fund housing for workers. It is levied at a rate of 0.45%
  of gross salaries, though this is reduced if the business invests in
  housing for its own employees.

In addition businesses pay annual company car tax on cars less than
ten years old of either €1,130 or €2,440. Vehicle tax is also payable on
lorries and heavy goods vehicles.

Social security contributions

In the case of employee directors who are minority or equal
shareholders of a *SARL*, social security contributions are levied on the
same basis as for other employees, save that they are not entitled to
unemployment benefits should then lose their job, and hence no
contributions are paid to Assedic. Majority director shareholders of a *SARL*
and proprietors of an *Entreprise Individuelle* are covered by the *régime
des non-salariés* (see below).

The social security bill for the *non-salarié*

Whilst in the past employees received a higher level of cover than the
self-employed, on the whole for retirement and illness cover this is no
longer the case. It remains true, however, for unemployment benefits. In
practice the total social security bill for the self-employed is lower than in
relation to employees.

The calculation is not straightforward. There are separate calculations
for the various kinds of social security cover, each with different rules. The
details are as follows:

* *La cotisation URSSAF*:
  the rate is 5.4% of taxable income (i.e. after deducting allowable
  business expenses);
* *La cotisation Maladie*:
  the rate is 5.9% of taxable income. There is a minimum amount payable
  (currently €845) whether the business is making a profit or not;

- *La cotisation Vieillesse*:
  the rate is 16.45% of taxable income. There is currently a minimum of €250;

- *La cotisation Invalidité-Décès*:
  the rate is 1.5% of taxable income with a minimum payment of just over €90;

- *La cotisation au régime complémentaire de retraite obligatoire*:
  the rate of 6.5%, with a minimum annual payment of just under €100.

In your first calendar year of business contributions are based on a fixed figure of notional profit that for 2005 was €6,365. This produces a total social security bill for year 1 of €2,345.40 for businesses starting on the 1st January. Obviously most businesses do not start on that date, and contributions are then based on a proportion of the year, depending when in the calendar year the business is started. For the second calendar year the notional figure for calculating contributions is 50% higher at €9,547, producing a contributions bill of €3,261.98. If the actual profits are less then these notional figures then you are entitled to request this be taken into account in calculating your liability. There is also an initial 90-day period during which no payment is requested, and it is also possible to apply to put off any payment of contributions until you have been in business for twelve months. Note that those in self-employment who also have an employed position must participate in both systems. Those in employment who are also setting up a new business can apply for an exemption from liability to pay self-employed contributions for the first twelve months of their business.

From year 3 onwards social security contributions are based on the profit levels of two years earlier. This can cause major problems for businesses in which profit levels fluctuate. A business that suffers a downturn in year five, for example, after a high level of profits in year three, will have to pay a large social security contribution in year five despite reduced revenue, and may accordingly experience severe cash flow problems. Indeed, in the first five years a business with a fluctuating profit level could pay significantly more than another business that has had a gradual but continual increase in profits. This can be the case even where the business with fluctuating profits has had a significantly lower total level of profit over those five years than the business with steady but continually increasing profits.

It is accordingly wise to put aside a substantial proportion of your profit each year as a provision against your future liabilities. It can be difficult to predict your future liability, but if you put aside one third of your annual profits this should generally be sufficient.

Employing staff

Vacancies can be filled via ANPE (www.anpe.fr) or using advertisements in the newspapers and web sites listed in Chapter 3. Employers are required to complete a *document unique d'embauche (DUE)* for each new employee. This is submitted to URSSAF, the body responsible for collection of social security contributions, and must be received by it at least eight days before the employee starts work. Employing staff is expensive. You should assume that the social contributions and other payments that you will be required to make will add an additional 60% of the employee's salary, though social security contributions are reduced by 26% in respect of employees receiving the minimum wage. The full level of contributions is payable once the employee's salary reaches 160% of the minimum wage.

There are also various incentive schemes for employing the long-term unemployed, the socially disadvantaged, the low-paid and the young or for taking on employees in disadvantaged areas that provide employers with exemptions or partial exemptions from social security contributions. For example employers taking on those who have been unemployed (and registered with the ANPE) for more than twelve months, receive state aid, known as *L'Aide Dégressive à l'Emploi*. This is payable over three years starting at 40% of the employee's salary for the first year, reducing to 30% in the second year and 20% in the third year, subject to a ceiling on the state's contribution equal to the amount of state benefits that the employee was receiving at the time he was taken on. It is also payable in relation to fixed term contracts of between 12 and 18 months, with 40% of the subsidy being paid during the first third of the contract, 30% in the second third etc. The qualifying period of unemployment is reduced to three months for those aged 50 and above.

Details of other financial incentives, including training schemes, and programmes to assist younger employees, are contained in Chapter 4.

Selling or closing down a business

Selling or closing down a business is rather more complicated than in the UK. To ensure that you comply with the correct procedures it is advisable to consult an *avocat* and an accountant. You will find that there are numerous steps to take in between the signing of the *compromis de vente* and the *acte de vente*. If you need to make staff redundant, this can be expensive. It is imperative to follow the correct procedure for *licenciement*, as a failure to do so could make the procedure even more costly. You should send all communications to staff by registered letter, even those you see on a daily basis. You are required to contact your creditors and obtain up to date statements of account showing how much you owe them. You should them settle these bills.

Similarly you must inform ASSEDIC and URSSAF, the VAT and various tax authorities. As always when dealing with French administration, it is advisable to go and see them, rather than deal with them just be telephone or post. Generally you will find staff more helpful and understanding if they have actually met you. Your accountant must prepare a final set of accounts. Once the tax authorities are satisfied that your tax affairs have been finalised, they will send you a *main levée*. A good place to obtain advice is your local Chamber of Commerce.

Chapter Seven

LIVING IN FRANCE

An uneasy *Entente Cordiale*

There are many Britons living in France and who have received a warm welcome from their French hosts. Some areas, such as Brittany, are particularly noted for their friendliness, whereas others have a reputation for giving the British a rather cool reaction, such as the Côte d'Azur. In relation to the latter region, however, it is fair to say that many of its residents originate from other parts of France, and that an unfriendly person that you encounter may not be a local at all, or indeed French! It is also worth remembering, that amongst the French themselves certain regions have a reputation for disliking the arrival of newcomers from other parts of France, let alone foreigners, and that in many areas there is considerable hostility towards Parisians purchasing holiday homes and driving up property prices.

On the whole, however, the French as a nation have a very ambivalent attitude to the English in particular, despite the hundred-year history of the *Entente Cordiale*. The attitude of the French media is typified by a news presenter that I often listen to, who I have heard refer to the Germans as *nos amis les Allemands*, when earlier that week he had referred to the English as *nos voisins les Anglais*. One cannot help feeling occasionally that the image of Joan of Arc seems more present in the French psyche, even today, than the two devastating world wars fought against their German neighbours. The French seem blissfully unaware that the fifteenth century wars between France and England were in reality a dispute within the royal families of France and England, which were both thoroughly French in any case, with the warriors of both armies speaking the French language, and not English. Indeed, the Duke of Burgundy supported the "English" candidature for the throne of France, and it was he who captured Joan of Arc and sold her to the English. The truth is that the English armies fighting in France were far less invaders than William the Conqueror, the French speaking Norman who seized the crown of England in 1066! For the English, the latter date is merely a date in history that we all learn at school, and to my knowledge at least conjures up no ill feeling towards our French friends and neighbours.

It is true, of course, than many English people do not help the image of our nation in France, ranging from the arrogant Englishman who expects to be understood if he shouts loud enough in English, to the well-healed louts who participated in the car race from London to Monaco endangering lives on their reckless journey, or the yobbish behaviour of English tourists in Ibiza that the French media seem to love to portray. It is perhaps not surprising that some of the French dislike the growing number of British arriving in their country, even though the number is far exceeded by Portuguese economic immigrants, and the arrivals from the former French north African colonies.

Feelings of hostility towards the English are much to do also with a resentment at the world dominance of English, a language which most French parents reluctantly acknowledge that their child should learn, and one which with the expansion of the EU has grown in importance even within Europe. Indeed, many young French nationals have moved to the UK, primarily to London were there are an estimated 300,000 French residents, but also to Manchester and other parts of the UK. They are attracted by the higher salaries, the opportunities for acquiring computer skills which are more advanced than in France, and the possibility of improving their level of English.

If you are Scottish, Welsh or Irish, you would do well to describe yourself as such, and avoid any reference to being British! Whilst many French do not fully understand the concept of the United Kingdom, and often confuse British with English, they generally reserve a warmer welcome for those of Celtic origin. One of the most popular British personalities in France is the Scottish yachtswoman Ellen MacArthur, one of the rare British personalities seen on French television to speak French with ease.

The faces of France

France is one of the world's largest economies, and most affluent countries. It has an excellent and efficient public transport network, a health system that delivers a high standard of care, and a volume car industry that puts the UK to shame. At the same time, it is a country that has developed very quickly, and still has rural areas that in many respects have remained unchanged, including in terms of attitudes. Parisians may have been extremely irritated about the picture of France portrayed in *A Year in Provence*, but that does not make that picture untrue, for Provence.

Whilst the French health system delivers an excellent service, with most British residents in France considering it superior to the British NHS, it is costing the country far too much. So too are the present pension arrangements. One international report disparagingly commented that the French do not appear to understand the need to plan (and pay) for the future. Unemployment is already at nearly 10%, and cuts still need to be made in the numbers employed in the public sector, which still accounts for a staggering 25% of the workforce.

It is also a country with substantial social problems and social tensions, and a large minority of nearly five million Muslims, primarily descendants of immigrants from France's former north-African colonies. For the most part they live in low quality housing estates on the outskirts of the country's main cities, and are unsurprisingly discontent with their lot. Following a consistent decline in the number of racist attacks in the 1990s, the last four years has seen a startling increase in the number of incidents, especially in Ile de France, Alsace, Corsica, and Rhône-Alpes. The main targets have been Jews, though north-Africans have also suffered. Recent years have seen pitched battles between gypsies and young Muslim men, and a large exodus of Jews in response to what is seen as a growing level of anti-semitism. Indeed the emigration of French Jews to Israel has caused a spiral of property prices in some parts of Israel.

French bureaucracy

Following its victory in the 2002 elections, the right wing government adopted goals to control public expenditure, reduce bureaucracy and enable businesses to prosper. A major target on the latter front has been the relaxation of the 35-hour week introduced by their socialist predecessors. The government's success in reducing spending and bureaucracy is more questionable. The French regularly complain about the bureaucracy of government bodies, and the arcane language so frequently used by the administration. The problem is so bad that publishers Robert have teamed up with the Ministry for State Reform to publish *Le Petit Décodeur des Mots de l'Administration en clair*. It contains about 3,000 terms expressed in everyday French. Cassell have produced a bilingual guide *The Cassell Guide to French Officialese*.

Good Europeans?

The British are frequently portrayed on French media as anti-European. Of course, there is some truth in this. However, it is worth remembering that France's record in implementing EU directives is in fact far worse than that of the UK, and that many people who wish to work in France have encountered resistance from the French authorities, especially in relation to the recognition of qualifications. The EU has now created an official organisation to handle such problems, with offices in all member states. You should contact the office in the UK. Contact details are available by telephoning 00 800 678 91011 or on the website www.europa.eu.int/solvit/site/centres/index_en.htm. The European Commission has also published a guide, *Dialogue with Citizens*, to assist

EU citizens who have encountered problems in relation to the exercise of their rights to live, work, travel and study anywhere within the EU. It explains how to challenge unfavourable decisions and how to use each member state's administrative and legal systems to obtain redress. The website is accessible via www.europa.eu.int. Go to Ploteus Portal and then 777777links.

Your right to stay in France

As a citizen of a member state of the European Union, you have the right to live and work in any other member state, including France. No special documentation is required for the first 90 days, save for a valid UK passport. You should carry your passport with you at all times. You will need it as a form of identification if you wish to pay by cheque. It can also be asked for at any time by a police officer.

Retiring to France

France is a favourite destination for those seeking to retire abroad, who are attracted by the climate (especially in coastal areas), the generally lower cost of housing, the lower cost of living (most notably in relation to fuel costs) and an efficient and user-friendly health service.

It is important to appreciate, however, that some who have moved to France have regretted the decision. They have found themselves isolated from their friends and family, and missing much of what they left behind in the UK. Those who become ill, or who lose their partner, or who with advancing age find it difficult to manage alone are particularly at risk. Careful thought needs to be given before making the move. There is a great deal to be said for moving to an area where you will find other British residents, such as the Côte d'Azur, the Dordogne, Poitou-Charentes and Brittany. In these areas you will find a wide range of facilities and services for the anglophone community, some of which are detailed in Chapter 1.

Remember that there are fewer care and nursing homes in France than in the UK, and limited care provision in the community. Save in a few areas, there is no equivalent to "*Meals on Wheels*" for example. The following web sites contain useful information for the elderly, including directories of homes, and some (limited) information in English: www.agevillage.com, www.maison-de-retraite.net, www.arepa.org (the web site of *L'Association des Résidences pour les Personnes Agées*).

One potential difficulty where the source of your income is in the UK, at least until the UK adopts the euro, is exchange rate fluctuations. One option is to move some of your investments to France. In any event you should ask your financial adviser about the possibility of doing this, should the value of sterling start to decline.

If you are considering retiring to France, you can obtain general advice from Age Concern, Astral House, 1268 London Road, London SW16 4ER Tel: 020 8765 7200. Other sources of advice are www.natpen.con.org.uk and www.seniorsworld.co.uk.

Receiving your pension in France

There is no difficulty in arranging for your state or private pension to be paid to you in France, and you are entitled to the same health rights as a French citizen. It is possible for those retiring early to receive health cover up to two and a half years prior to the standard date of retirement. The retired receive full reimbursement of medical expenses. For further information, see the practical guide – *Your Rights when moving within the European Union* available on the web site www.europa.eu.int/comm/employment_social/index. Go to *Co-ordination of social security schemes* (under *Working conditions and working organisations*) and then see *The Community provisions on social security: Your Rights when moving within the European Union*. You can also contact the DWP (tel: 0191 2187777) and ask for a copy of their leaflet SA29. They should also supply you with form E121 so that you can register with the French health services. Those who have not yet retired should be given an E106. In either case, take the form to the local health office in France who should provide you with a French medical card.

For details of recent changes in UK pensions see the web site www.thepensionservice.gov.uk or telephone (00 44 191 2182828) and ask for the leaflet "*Your State Pension Choice – Pension now or extra pension later: a Guide to State Pension deferral*".

Those still working have their existing entitlement to a UK pension frozen and will receive a reduced pension from the UK authorities at retirement age. For those approaching retirement, it may be worthwhile making voluntary payments to bring your National Insurance contributions up to the level entitling you to a full pension. You should contact The Pension Service's International Pension Centre (part of the Department for Work and Pensions on tel: 0191 218 7777) and the Inland Revenue's Centre for Non-Residents (tel: 0845 070 0040). Ask for up-to-date information and advice, including whether you should pay Class 2 or Class 3 contributions. The former is the more expensive option but entitles you to incapacity benefit.

Other UK benefits

You are entitled to receive other benefits such as invalidity and disability benefits, widows' benefits or benefits received as a result of an accident at work, or an occupational disease, wherever you live. The payments should be made gross. Those living within the EU will also benefit from increases in the level of payment. Incapacity benefit is only paid to those who have paid Class 1 or Class 2 and 4 National Insurance contributions.

As to unemployment benefit, those out of work are entitled to have the Jobseeker's Allowance paid to them in France for up to 13 weeks. You must have been registered as a job seeker for at least four weeks before you left the UK, and have been available for work up until your departure. You must be leaving the UK in search of work, and register as seeking work with the French authorities within seven days of your last claim for Jobseeker's Allowance in the UK. You must contact your Jobcentre Plus office or Jobcentre before leaving, and complete the appropriate forms if you have not done so already to claim benefit. You should be sent a copy of E303 before you leave to enable you to claim benefit in France, and form E119 to entitle you to health care. If you cannot find employment during that 13-week period, then you will have to return to the UK if you wish to continue to receive benefit. You are only entitled to claim Job Seeker's Allowance abroad for one 13-week period between periods of employment. Information on transferring your Job Seeker's Allowance is contained in leaflet JSAL 22 available from your local DWP office.

Non-means tested UK child benefit can still be claimed by those who live in France, but who remain liable for and are paying UK income tax and National Insurance contributions.

You should obtain the leaflet SA29 "Your Social Security, Insurance, Benefits and Health Care Rights in the European Community", by contacting the Department for Work and Pensions (International Services) at Longbenton, Newcastle-Upon-Tyne NE98 1YX Tel: 0191 225 4811, www.dwp.gov.uk. A further leaflet worth asking form is the guide "Social Security for Migrant Workers" available from the Department for Work and Pensions, Pensions and Overseas Benefits Directorate, Tyneview Park, Whitley Road, Benton, Newcastle-upon-Tyne NE98 1BA 0191 2187777.

Your rights to French state benefits

If you are working and paying tax and social security contributions in France, you may become entitled to claim state benefits in France. The national insurance contributions that you have paid in the UK will be taken into account in determining your entitlement. The rate of unemployment benefit is pegged at three quarters of the minimum wage, namely around €340 per month. There is also a system of income support, the RMI, *le revenu minimum d'insertion*.

There are various maternity benefits, and benefits payable to parents following a birth or adoption, and annual payments each September to purchase school equipment. Additional payments are made to parents with children who are not in work, single parents, and parents of handicapped children or children with special needs.

Importing your belongings (for motor vehicles see Chapter 11)

EU citizens are entitled to bring all personal belongings with them to France, though naturally there are restrictions governing items such as drugs and firearms, animals, animal products, plants and items with a possible military use. If you are in any doubt, verify the position with French customs beforehand.

Pets

European regulations provide that to take a dog or cat to France it must be identified with a microchip, then vaccinated against rabies and issued with a pet passport (in that order). The latter will contain details about the animal and its owner, in particular the date it was microchipped and details of vaccinations. Similar rules apply to ferrets. In the UK a passport is obtained from a vet authorised to issue them. The Department for Environment Food and Rural Affairs (DEFRA) runs a Pets Helpline 08459 335577, and has an informative and regularly updated web site www.defra.gov.uk. There is a link to enable you to download a passport form. The site www.eurotunnel.com also includes information relating to pets.

You are required to accompany your pet or meet it at the port of entry. If your dog or cat is under three months old, it can be taken to France before vaccination, but must have a passport. In addition, you must be able to certify that it has remained at the same location since birth and either that it has had no contact with wild animals that are likely to have been exposed to rabies, or that it is still dependent on its mother and is accompanied by her.

Matters are more difficult when it comes to bringing your dog or cat back cat into the UK. The regulations are identical to those above, but the UK authorities also require that your animal must have a blood test to check that the vaccine has been effective. This cannot be taken until at least one month after the vaccination, after which you must then wait for a further six months before your pet is permitted to enter the UK. You would be well advised to allow about eight months in all. Before you send the sample for testing verify with the test centre how long they take to return results, as this can vary widely. In addition, 24-48 hours before leaving for the UK your dog or cat must be treated for ticks and tapeworm. You will find a list of companies that are authorised to transport pets into the UK in the Appendices, and can find an up-to-date list on the DEFRA web site that will include those recently added. There are similar provisions in relation to the importation of ferrets into the UK, save that there is no six month waiting period.

There are currently no restrictions on guinea pigs, hamsters, rats, mice and gerbils entering either France or the UK, though there are regulations governing other animals, such as birds (other than poultry), ornamental tropical fish, most invertebrates, and reptiles. You should consult the DEFRA web site for further information in relation to these.

There are transitional arrangements that allow pets issued with UK PETS certificates issued up until 30.09.04 that are still valid to enter both the UK and France, though the certificate can be exchanged for a pet's passport (consult your veterinary surgeon).

Dog owners in France should vaccinate their dog against hepatitis, parvoviris, leptospirosis, distemper, kennel cough and also leishmaniasis, as well as ensure that they receive an annual rabies injection. Cats should be vaccinated against feline leukaemia and feline enteritis. Health insurance is available for pets. Insurance against accidents will cost around €80 per year. A policy that also covers illness will cost you about twice as much. Note that different policies contain widely different exclusions and most only pay a proportion of the veterinary costs.

French law provides that within France all dogs born after 06.01.99 must be registered with an official identifying number – either a tattoo in their ear, or a microchip inserted beneath the skin (usually in their neck). Tattooing is carried out under an anaesthetic. No anaesthetic is required for the insertion of a microchip. A microchip can be painlessly inserted. Several vets have informed me that microchips do not cause any irritation to your dog. Whether your dog receives a microchip or a tattoo, you should also attach a nametag with your contact details to its collar.

If you have lost or found a pet you should inform the register responsible (01 49 37 54 54 for dogs, and 01 55 01 08 08 for cats). If your animal is tattooed or has a microchip then the chances of you being reunited with your pet are obviously much higher. If you have lost a pet contact your local *mairie* and ask where to find the local pound (*fourrière*). You may also derive assistance from the local branch of the SPA, (*Société Protectrice des Animaux* www.spa.asso.fr). For details of kennels see the web site www.royalcanin.fr (tel: 0800 415161), and for general information (in English) see www.dogsaway.co.uk.

Losing property on the beach, in your garden, in a field

If you lose an item of value, or a set of car keys, in the sand, or in your garden, consider turning to *L'Association Française des prospecteurs* (tel: 01 43 07 55 99). This is a free service staffed by enthusiastic volunteers armed with metal detectors.

Opening and running a bank account in France

When you open an account you will be provided with a chequebook (with your address printed on each cheque) and *carte bleue*. The latter is used for making withdrawals from cash machines. You can also use it as a payment card using your code. Cheques remain a very popular means of payment in France, being twenty more times used than in the UK. You will need to produce your passport when issuing a cheque. Post-dating a cheque is ineffective - it can be drawn on immediately. Note that your bank will give you a limit on how much you can withdraw each month, and you will not be able to use your *carte bleue* as a payment card if you exceed this limit, even if you have funds in your account.

Bank charges in France are still higher than in most other European countries, even for routine operations. However, they are no longer permitted to make a charge for closing an account, and following a recent decision of the European Court of Justice they must now pay interest on current accounts (though as no requirement was laid down as to how much interest, the rates are likely to be modest). Following government pressure, 2005 has seen the banks taking measures to make their charges more transparent. According to the web site www.testepourvous.com one of the cheapest banks is in fact *La Poste* with BNP Paribas also offering a good value service. Commission on transfers out of France vary tremendously. If you are likely to make regular transfers abroad, a bank's charges for this service should be one of the factors you consider when deciding upon your choice of bank. Becoming overdrawn or exceeding an overdraft limit without prior agreement is a serious matter in France and should be avoided! As with other banks, notify your French bank immediately of any loss or suspected theft of your chequebook or card. You are responsible for any loss until you do.

Complaints about banking services should first be addressed to the local manager. Banks are now required to appoint a *médiateur*. You can issue euro cheques whilst in another EU country, providing the payee agrees, though you may both have to pay bank charges for this. The position is likewise if you accept a euro cheque from another EU country. Cheques in France remain valid for one year and eight days. Post-dating cheques is not permissible. Those resident in France may not use more than €3,000 cash to purchase any goods or service, but must use a cheque or card. A professional who accepts a larger cash payment can be fined up to €15,000.

You can only stop a cheque (*faire opposition*) if it has been lost or stolen. You will need to telephone 08 92 683208. You will then need to confirm this by writing to your bank. Either hand the letter to a cashier, or send it by letter *avec accusé de réception*.

It is extremely unwise to issue a cheque *sans provision* (i.e. without funds in your account). Such a cheque is often referred to as a *chèque en bois* (wooden cheque). The cheque will be returned to the payee who will ask for some other means of payment. If the payee does not receive payment within 30 days he is entitled to obtain a *certificat de non paiement* from the bank. The payee can then send this to the issuer of the cheque by letter *avec accusé de réception*. Once the payee has done this he can ask a *huissier* to contact the issuer, who if necessary can have the money deducted from the issuer's salary, or arrange for his goods to be seized and sold. The costs of this procedure are added to the amount owed to the payee.

Those who have issued such cheques will find that their account will be frozen until they have put sufficient funds in the account and the payee has re-presented the cheque. Alternatively the issuer can pay the debt in some other way, but will need to give the original cheque to his bank. The issuer must pay the payee within two months or face a fine. The issuer of a bounced cheque also has to pay additional bank charges per cheque wrongly issued, plus fines if they have bounced more than three cheques in a 12-month period. The fines are substantial – 33% of the value of each cheque over €50.

It should not be possible to open or operate any other bank account in this period - the issuer's bank notifies the *Banque de France* which will then list the issuer in its database of defaulters. If the issuer does not pay the amount he owes, plus the fines, he will remain on the list for five years during which he is subject to an *interdiction bancaire* when his access to banking facilities is significantly restricted, in particular in relation to the use of cheques.

If you believe that you might go overdrawn or exceed your overdraft limit (*découvert*) contact the person responsible for your account immediately. He or she may be able to provide you with short-term assistance.

You will often be asked for your RIB or *relevé d'identité bancaire*, for example if you are taking out a credit transaction requiring regular deductions from your bank account. You will also find that utility bills have a detachable slip with the identical details to those on your RIB, which you simply sign and return to enable the payee to have the sum deducted from your bank account. There is much to be said for paying by direct debit, particularly if you are away from the property for extended periods.

Notify your bank as soon as possible if you lose your chequebook or card, or suspect that it has been stolen. If you comply with this requirement your liability should be limited to €150. As yet there is no overall number that you can telephone to arrange for cancellation of all your cards, though Card Protection Plus have a policy that will include both your French and British cards (see their web site www.cpp.co.uk).

British banks (of which there are a number in France, including Barclays with a substantial network) are governed by the same rules as French banks.

Taking and transferring money to France

There are no difficulties in making transfers from your UK account to a French account. Transfers can take two or three working days to arrive, though in practice I have found that my French account is generally credited the same or the next working day. Under new European regulations the receiving bank is not allowed to make a charge for receiving sums in euros. Your UK bank may make a charge of €20—30 per transfer, irrespective of the amount. Changing to a French bank that is part of the same group as your UK bank may significantly reduce the charge. Ensure that you obtain the commercial rate for transfers. This is much more favourable than the tourist rate. Bank charges generally also vary and it accordingly pays to shop around.

Offshore banking

The laws of both France and the UK require residents to pay tax on their *world-wide* income. In the past many people have evaded income tax on unearned income by keeping assets in off shore bank accounts. The new EU Savings Tax Directive is aimed at preventing this. It is to be implemented across Europe, including the Isle of Man and the Channel Islands. The directive applies to interest earned on bank deposits, interest from certain bonds, and income from certain types of investment funds. In brief banks have a choice either to levy a withholding tax on their customers, or to provide the tax authorities in your country of residence with information relating to the interest earned on your account. For the most part, banks are permitting their customers to decide which of the two options should be selected. The current rate of withholding tax is 15%, but is set to rise from July 2008 to 20%, and from July 2011 to 35%. Those who are already paying tax on such income will need to choose the exchange of information option to avoid being taxed twice.

Insurance

In France it is compulsory to insure your home. It is also obligatory to have insurance for public liability, including for your child at school. Most comprehensive policies (*assurances multirisques habitation*) include public liability. Your belongings, and your home should be insured to their full value, otherwise any claim will only be met in part. For property allow for the cost of the land, demolition and rebuilding. Inform your insurers if the property is to be empty for prolonged periods and if you are renting the property out. They may levy a higher premium, but if you do not inform them you risk a claim on the policy being disallowed.

Time limits for making a claim are very short, and you should check the terms of the policy. It will normally also require you to report thefts and break-ins to the police within 24 hours. Failure to do so could result in a refusal to satisfy a claim.

Contracts of insurance are automatically renewable, and accordingly should you fail to pay the annual premium on time you should still be covered. On the other hand, if you wish to move to a different insurance company, you are generally required to give your existing company notice before the policy comes up for renewal.

La Protection Juridique

This is a *must*. For less than €50 a year you can have immediate access to a lawyer to ask any legal question, ranging from the purchase of a faulty consumer item, to problems with a noisy neighbour, to out of date gift vouchers. Furthermore, if you need to defend a claim against you, or wish to bring a claim against someone else, the cover may include funding this for you, saving you huge amounts in legal fees. Different policies have different types of cover, and you should ensure that you purchase a policy that is fairly wide. Obviously it is imperative that you can fully express yourself to the lawyer over the telephone, and understand his or her responses. If you need help the lawyer may speak English, alternatively enlist the assistance of someone with a good knowledge of French.

Heating your home

Your heating needs will depend upon a number of factors, including where you are living, the size and age of your home etc. Your choices will also be influenced by whether you are renting or have purchased your home, and the existing heating arrangements. Obviously, if you live in an apartment, you may have little or no choice. For convenience, electricity is ideal. It is frequently the choice for smaller flats and coastal properties in the south of France. Inexpensive to install, electricity is often chosen by landlords of single dwellings. The purchase of an electric heater that can simply be plugged into a socket is also an ideal for an occasional additional or emergency source of heating. The one drawback with electricity, however, is that the running costs are high.

Most properties in the cities and larger towns are connected to the mains gas supply, and can take advantage of the lower cost of gas. In the more rural areas, many people use bottled butane gas, often for cooking. This is relatively inexpensive, and can be delivered to your door. The rubber tubing, which should have an expiry date on it, should be checked regularly for cracks. Gas appliances are inefficient and dangerous if not functioning properly.

You can obtain advice on how best to heat your home, pollution and grants and subsidies available for using renewable fuels from ADEME – Agence de l'Environnement et la Maîtrise de l'Energie Tel : 0800 310 3111 www.ademe.fr For a charge of about €300 the agency will supply you with a written assessment of your energy needs, and detailed costings of the various options.

Carbon monoxide poisoning is not uncommon in France, and can cause headache, fatigue, nausea and problems with vision and hearing. It is a colourless, odourless gas, produced by the combustion of gas, oil, wood and coal. All too often sufferers do not connect what are quite common symptoms with gas poisoning. The escape of gas normally occurs because on appliance is faulty or incorrectly connected. Gas appliances need to be regularly serviced and maintained.

Solar energy

Energy from the sun is extremely economical, with minimal running costs, and a life span for a system of at least twenty years. It is becoming increasingly popular in the south of France, where it is possible for a solar system to satisfy most of your requirements for heating water and space. The major drawback is the high installation costs. A water-heating system (*chauffe eau-solaire individuel* or CESI) costs in the region of €3,800 to €5,500 to install, and a comprehensive system (*système solaire combiné*) for heating space as well as water, will cost between €13,000 and €22,000.

The French government is committed to encouraging the use of renewable heat resources. Its previously generous system of subsidies, however, has now been replaced with a system of a tax credits covering up to 40% of the cost but limited to principal residences. There remain a number of grants and subsidies available from local and regional authorities (primarily *Conseils Régionaux* and certain *Conseils Généraux* and *Communes*).

Tax relief and grants are only available to those using a certified installer (*agréé qualisol*), and an approved system. The installers can provide you with up to date assistance on the funding available, and the options for hire-purchase. Qualisol logo installers have committed themselves to a charter setting out standards, and are subject to random controls and inspections. You can find a list of certified Qualisol installers on the ADEME web site (*Base des Entreprises Qualisol*), and in the Yellow Pages under *Energies solaires*.

A second disadvantage of a solar system is that you cannot rely on the sun for your energy throughout the year. Accordingly you will need a back up provision. In many cases portable electrical heaters will be sufficient.

Air-conditioning

Increasingly modern buildings have the benefit of air-conditioning, a great relief during the height of summer. If the property is without this facility, it may be worthwhile obtaining an estimate, especially if you are purchasing a new home. Note that for older people, some form of system for lowering the temperature is likely to be essential, and if there is no central air conditioning, serious consideration should be given to obtaining a portable gas cooler.

Electricity bills

Your electricity bill will be determined by the level of power supply and the type of tariff selected, in addition to your consumption of electricity. As to the power supply (measured in kilowatt-hours (kWh)), this could be as low as 3.3 kWh for a small flat with only basic electrical equipment. For a larger house, and for those running a washing machine, dishwasher and electric cooker, a supply of between 9 and 18~kWh will be necessary. For family homes in which several electrical appliances are likely to be operating simultaneously you should consider making an appointment with a representative of EDF (*Electricité de France*). The items that consume the most are water heaters, electric plates, washing machines, tumble-driers, dishwashers and kettles. Using all these items simultaneously adds up to a consumption of nearly 20 kWh, and if this is likely to happen in your household, you should consider having power up to 36 kWh.

EDF offers three different rates: *l'option base*, *l'option heures creuses* and *l'option tempo*. The *option* base is a simple flat rate. For *l'option heures creuses* there is a higher subscription charge, but you are able to benefit from a lower tariff for eight hours a day during the off-peak period. This is generally 1.00 a.m. to 7.30 a.m. and 12.30 p.m. to 2.00 p.m., although in many case EDF will allow some alteration in these times.

Those with holiday homes should consider opting for EDF's *tempo tariff* – you pay a much lower rate per kwh, for most days of the year (*jours bleus*). The catch is that you pay a higher rate on 43 days of the year (*jours blancs*) and a very much higher rate on 22 high peak days (*jours rouges*). The white and red days are between November and March, and are pre-selected and published by EDF. It is possible to have a warning system incorporated to alert you in advance of an imminent change in the tariff, and/or for the system to be automatically switched off at these times.

Note that power cuts are not uncommon in France, and you should consider fitting an uninterrupted power supply with a backing battery. You should also consider purchasing a power surge protector (at a cost of about €18) to avoid damage to electrical appliances during storms.

Where there is an interruption to your supply of electricity, but neighbouring properties are unaffected, EDF/GDF undertake to attend to the problem within four hours of your call. The same undertaking is given in relation to gas, though in urgent cases a representative will attend immediately. EDF/GDF can be contacted by telephoning the number that appears in the top left hand corner of your electricity bill, or on 0810 126 126 for EDF and 0810 140 159 for GDF (see also www.edf.fr and www.gazdefrance.fr). They publish leaflets in English explaining their services and charges.

Reduced charges for electricity, water and telephone

Following an agreement reached between the government and operators, those residing in France who benefit from RMI (*Revenu Minimum d'Insertion*) or who have a recognised handicap, receive discounted rates for subscriptions for electricity, water and telephone. Further information is available from your *mairie*.

Water bills

For the most part mains water supplies in France are metered. Prices vary according to the region, but bills can be quite hefty. An average family can easily use about 500 litres of water per day. About 60 per cent of an average family's consumption relates to the taking of baths and showers and the flushing of the cistern. Taking a shower consumes around a third of the quantity of water used in taking a bath. Modern toilet cisterns use a third or less of the amount used by older cisterns. Ensure that you cure all leaks – a leaking tap can consume up to 50,000 litres of water a year! Always ascertain where the main stop-valve or stopcock is located in case you need to turn off the water supply in an emergency. To check for leaks, take a meter reading last thing at night, and another first thing in the morning, taking care not to use the water supply in the meantime. If the meter indicates any significant consumption, then this suggests a leak is likely somewhere in the system. In most areas tap water is drinkable, though most people in France still preferred bottled water.

The telephone

To arrange for a connection, telephone 1014. To be ex-directory, ask to be included in the *liste rouge*. If you wish to avoid your details being included on mailing lists ask to be added to the *liste orange*. For general information see France Telecom's web site www.francetelecom.com. France Telecom operates a full range of services, including the reception of UK TV through your telephone line.

There are a number of operators offering quite attractive rates for expatriates, including AS24 Telecom, Phonexpat, Teleconnect, UK Telecom and IC Telecom Services. I personally have found Andy Martin of AS24 Telecom (andymartin@as24telecom.com) particularly helpful in explaining the different ways in which the companies calculate their charges, with some companies being very competitive if the majority of your calls are quite short, but far less competitive if your calls tend to be longer.

Telephone numbers commencing with 0805 are free. Those with a prefix of 0820 cost €0.12 per minute, those commencing by 0891 cost €0.30 per minute, and those starting with 0899 cost €0.75 per minute. Telephone 12 for Directory Enquiries, and 3212 for International Enquiries (though this is about to change with new multiple numbers being introduced starting with 118, as in the UK). To prevent the person you are calling from knowing your number, ring 3651 before they answer. To find out the number of the last person to telephone you, ring 3131. *Le Transfert d'Appel* allows you to transfer your calls to another land line or mobile telephone, for example whilst you are on holiday. France Telecom now have an English speaking service (free phone 0800 364 775). See also their web site at www.francetelecom.com/en/tools/others/contactus.html. It is well worth glancing at the information pages contained in *Les Pages Jaunes* – the details they contain are very useful.

With *la Ligne Résidence Secondaire* you can suspend your telephone line of your holiday home for up to six times a year. You keep the same telephone number and pay no line rental when the line is not activated. Each time you suspend the line you pay a fee of just under €5, with no charge for reactivation of the line. If you rent out premises you can take advantage of *Téléséjour* where the line remains activated to receive calls, but calls out are limited to emergency and free numbers.

Mobile telephones

There is a wide choice of mobile telephone providers, and you can now change provider whilst retaining your existing number. Hundreds of thousands of mobile telephones are stolen each year in France. Consider obtaining insurance cover for both the telephone, and in relation to the expensive collection of calls a thief is likely to make. Keep a record of your mobile phone identification code (it should be beside the battery). If your telephone is stolen, notify your operator immediately, as well as your insurer and the police. The relevant operator telephone numbers are Orange 0825 00 5700; Bouygues 0800 291000; and SFR 06 10001900.

Mobile telephone contracts remain automatically renewed on their expiry, but now the mobile phone company must notify you within one to three months of the renewal date, thereby reminding you of your right not to renew.

The postal system and services

La Poste is generally efficient. Most letters are delivered next day, with letters to the UK taking two to five working days. I have sent and received many parcels from the UK over the six years that I have lived in France. Occasionally there have been delays, but to my knowledge none has gone missing. It is nevertheless unwise to include cash in envelopes. In addition to first and second class post (prioritaire and économique), La Poste offers the following options for posting your letters and parcels:

- *Lettre Suivie* - enables you to ascertain the date your letter arrived

- *Lettre Recommandée* - avec Avis de Réception (AR) this provides you with a proof of posting, notification of reception of your letter at its destination with a signature from the recipient of your letter, and compensation if your letter is lost. This service is generally chosen when sending official or important documents

- *Colissimo* - this consists of several different services for the sending of packages. For the most part the sender receives a proof of sending, can ascertain when it was received, and is entitled to compensation if the packet is lost. Delivery is made within two working days of posting, and there is an option for obtaining the signature of the recipient. This service is substantially cheaper than chronopost (see below). You can purchase special packaging from the post-office.

- *Chronopost* - this service provides you with proof of posting, a signature by the recipient, a notification of reception, compensation in the event of the loss of the parcel, and a guarantee of delivery the next working day before 12.00 midday. You can obtain special packaging from the post-office.

- *Les Prêts-à-Poster* - these are pre-paid envelopes for letters and parcels that you purchase in advance, with various weight limits for parcels up to 2 kg. The envelopes are free of charge, and for parcels are very strong and come with an inner bubble-wrap bag. A major advantage is that you do not have to queue to post the envelope – if it will not fit in the letter box, simply go to the front of the queue and hand it to a member of the counter staff. From time to time a discount is offered if you purchase three or ten envelopes for parcels. *Les Prêt-à-Poster* are treated as first class post. Parcels to the UK often arrive within two working days, but can take three or four.

La Poste has introduced an electronic version of the registered letter, *la lettre recommandée électronique*. It can be sent at any time of day or night. It is printed out by *La Poste*, and then delivered in the usual way. The cost is €6.24 per page. For further information see www.laposte.fr.LRE, and also the useful information on this subject on www.skovgaard-europe.com

If you wish to have post redirected to your new address, in France or abroad, this can be done for a period of six months. Ask for a *Contrat de Réexpédition ou de Garde du Courrier* from your local post office.

Most post-offices are open from 08.00 to 18.00 Monday to Friday and Saturday morning. The main post-offices generally remain open over lunchtime. Fax and Minitel services are available in most branches, as is an automated service for weighing and paying for letters and parcels. The latter is extremely user friendly, and can be used in English. You can, of course, also obtain stamps from a *tabac*.

Television and satellite

There are several French television channels. The following rules apply to French television:

- programmes frequently start up to ten minutes before or after the advertised time;
- series and serials often end abruptly without any warning, either on the television channel itself, or in the TV magazines;
- transmissions are frequently interrupted. If this happens, no indication is given as to how long it will last, nor what the cause was, nor is any apology offered. When transmission is resumed, you may be watching another programme, and never know the outcome of the thriller than you had been watching for the previous hour and a half;
- repeats are common, especially of children's cartoons.

If any of the above occurs, do not adjust your set.

A licence fee is payable per house or apartment in which there is a television set. It is payable irrespective of whether you watch French television, i.e. even if you only use the set to view satellite television channels. When you purchase a television, the vendor is obliged to notify the authorities to enable them to collect the licence fee. From 2005 the *redevance télé* is collected with the *taxe d'habitation*. No fee is payable by those aged 65 and over if they were exempt from income tax for the previous year, nor by those with a disability of 80% or more providing they earned less than around €7,200.

Many foreign residents prefer to receive English language programmes. There are a number of options for receiving UK TV and radio programmes via satellite. Some channels can be received free of charge using a receiver that you can purchase from a dealer or electrical retailer. Britons in France receive BBC 1, BBC 2, ITV, Channel 4, Channel 5 and Sky by using a receiver available from specialists and a card from the UK. This is, in fact, unlawful as licensing and copyright laws restrict the use of the card to the UK. A list of suppliers and installers of satellite equipment is included in Appendix 1.

Internet

There are a number of service providers, including wanadoo (France Telecom) and AOL. ADSL compares favourably with Broadband in the UK, and is generally cheaper and no slower than in the UK. For a comparison of ADSL prices in France visit www.ariase.com/fr/observatoire/fai/adsl.html, and for a comparison of dial up rates see www.ariase.com/fr/observatoire/fai/56.html. Over a third of French communes now have complete ADSL coverage. To check whether your commune has it you can consult the site www.degrouptest.com. A list of Internet vocabulary is included in the Appendices.

The railway system

French trains run on time. They are publicly owned and efficient. The TGV reaches 250 km/h. You can purchase tickets with a credit card by telephoning 0892 353535, and find out train times by ringing 0891 676869. For further information see the web site www.sncf.com.

Help and assistance

There are numerous groups and associations of English-speakers, especially in the larger cities, the Dordogne and the popular coastal areas, and many of them offer advice and a friendly welcome to newcomers. You will find details of many of these associations on the web sites of www.anglo.info.com that now has sites for the Riviera, Provence, Normandy, Brittany, and Poitou-Charentes. Lists of associations are also kept by the British consulates (see Appendix 1 for their contact details). The British Association has a large number of branches throughout France, and in the right circumstances will even provide financial assistance to British citizens in need. Another group with a wide membership is the Association France-Grande-Bretagne (183 avenue Daumesnil, 75012 Paris, tel: 0155787171). In Paris many English-speakers often use the facilities, including notice boards, of the British Council. In the capital there is also an organisation called SOS Help (tel: 01 46 214646; www.soshelpline.org) that provides counselling in English.

In most of the larger cities and in the more popular areas there are Anglican Churches. Their contact details can be found on www.anglicansonline.org.uk (go to "Europe", "Diocese in Europe", "Chaplancies Location" and lastly to "France". Details of churches from other denominations can be obtained from your nearest British Consulate. You can also try www.angloinfo.com and the web site of *French News*, www.french-news.com.

Two other organisations of note are *Adapt in France* and *Accueil des Villes Françaises* (AVF). The former is designed to assist primarily English speakers. It is based on the Riviera, and holds numerous workshops on different aspects of life in France, and has a library of useful resources. Membership fees start at around €50. The web site is at www.adaptinfrance.org (tel: 0493653379). AVF is a long-established association with branches in most cities and larger towns. It welcomes all newcomers to the town, offering advice and assistance. It is also open to those who have moved into the town within the last few years. Branches of AVF hold social events, and often have a considerable range of "clubs" or classes attached, ranging from French classes, to chess, to hiking. It is a good way to meet French people, although there are a considerable number of foreigners also amongst its members.

Becoming part of the community

Joining an organisation such as the local branch of the AVF (see above) is certainly one way of quickly making contacts in the local community. If you have children at school, you will find that they make friends and that you will be meeting other parents through them, as well as at the various school events. The French are often very stiff and formal, and you may well need to take the initiative yourself. Participation in local sports and cultural associations is another means of becoming part of the local community. You should also introduce yourself to your neighbours, including before you move into a property, and ask them about the local area. Buy the local newspapers, and try to do *some* of your shopping locally, even though it may be more expensive than at the nearest hypermarket.

Anglo-Saxons often find the French rather formal. This is certainly true in business and official correspondence, and many French people purchase books advising on how to present letters, containing precedent letters for a wide range of circumstances. It may take some time before your French neighbours drop *Monsieur or Madame* in favour of your Christian name. Avoid calling on your French friends and neighbours uninvited. It is preferable to telephone them first and ask if it is convenient to drop round.

Speaking and learning the language

If you are serious about integrating into France and becoming part of the community, or even feeling completely confident in your day-to-day encounters with French people and being able to deal with emergency situations, it is essential that you develop your ability to speak and to understand the French language. There are numerous possibilities available, including free or inexpensive courses run through the local unemployment office (ANPE) for those in search of work, the local branch of the AVF (see above), and often the local *mairie*. In some areas, such as parts of Brittany, courses have been introduced specifically designed for the British newcomers. Ideally you should start learning the language prior to moving to France, perhaps by attending a night class. Some of the best courses are those held by the French Institute that has centres in London and Manchester (see Appendix 1), *L'Alliance Française* (www.alliancefr.org) or through *La Maison Française* of which there are several centres in the UK, including at Oxford. These cultural centres provide you with an opportunity to meet French people, and to learn more about France and French culture.

Once in France there is a whole range of different courses, many of which are listed at The French Directory: Learn in France at www.europa-pages.com. Often these courses are completely in French, with no English at all. Those who wish to obtain qualifications can study for O level and A level French via correspondence courses with the National Extension College. There is also an External Degree in French Studies at London University, and a diploma in French with the Open University and a degree in Modern Languages Studies. The French authorities also have examinations to ascertain the level of foreigners French (such as the *Diplôme d'Etude de la Langue Française*), and you may wish to set this as a goal for yourself at some stage.

It is imperative to use your French as much as you can, and making French friends is the easiest and most economical way to learn the language. Naturally, those with a French partner gain maximum exposure to the language. Ensure that you watch French television. Do not be over ambitious in your viewing selection, at least not at the outset. The most difficult programmes to follow are heated debates – the participants all talk at the same time, and the presenters do not have anywhere near the control over the discussion that is exercised by British presenters of such shows. French films are also often difficult to follow, in that they frequently take for granted a knowledge of French life and society, and contain a large amount of slang that is difficult to pick up.

Consider watching some of the children's cartoons – obviously if you have young children you have the perfect excuse to do this. *Les Petites Bêtes* is endearing and not too difficult to follow. The same is true of *Franklin* and *Cédric* (which I particularly recommend). *La Famille Pirate* and *Titeuf* are also worth watching, though more difficult, and in the latter case will contain some vocabulary that is somewhat cruder than is usual in cartoons on British television! Films and TV series translated from English are much easier to follow, in that for the most part they avoid the more colloquial slang, seldom use French regional accents, and do not assume a knowledge of French society, institutions, culture etc. News bulletins are also easier to follow as newsreaders usually speak fairly clearly.

Relations with your neighbours

It is always wise to introduce yourself to your neighbours with a view to establishing a good relationship with them. In the months or years to come, you may well need to call on each other for help. It is good to have someone nearby to turn to, for example if your car breaks down, or the electricity supply is suddenly interrupted. If an argument does arise with your neighbours you should endeavour to sort it out between yourselves, or by asking a neutral third party to act as an arbiter. Litigation is sometimes unavoidable, but it is expensive, stressful, and seldom provides either party with the result they had hoped for. It should definitely be a means of last resort! If you need to make contact with an absent neighbour, then the first port of call is to make enquiries at your local *mairie*.

There are rules governing noise levels, pollution and other nuisances. Your right to complain, however, is generally limited to abnormal nuisances, and not those that have been present in the area for many years, such as the erecting of local market stalls that disturbs your sleep from 6.00 a.m, as these are simply aspects of the neighbourhood with which you have to put up. Noise levels of 30 dB (decibels) above the normal background noise are illegal and can be punished with a fine of up to €450. You can obtain advice on neighbour disputes form the Association de Défense des Victimes de Troubles du Voisinage, 8, allée de la Forêt 78170 La Celle-Saint-Cloud Tel: 01.39.69.26.88. See also the web site www.bruit.fr. If you decide to make a formal complaint, or instigate court proceedings you should gather evidence, including with the help of videos and recording devices. You should keep a diary of important incidents, and ask others to make statements to support your case. The first step, after polite requests have been ignored, is to send a letter to the perpetrator of the nuisance by recorded delivery (*lettre recommandée avec avis de réception*). Your next port of call, if that fails, is to approach the local police, and/or the *mairie*. Consider instructing an avocat to advise you.

Les Immeubles en Fête is an annual event started in 1999 whereby those living in urban areas can get to know their neighbours. Organisers claim that 2 million residents participate each year.

Cutting back trees and vegetation

France introduced measures to counteract fire risks during the summer season. Property owners and occupiers must cut back trees and vegetation (*le débroussaillement*) within a radius of 50 metres of property. In areas most at risk this law is supplemented by further regulations introduced at a local level (for further details see www.ofme.org; www.debrouissaillement.com).

The police

A municipal police officer has only limited powers. If he believes that an offence has been committed he can ask for your name, but he is not entitled to require you to produce your ID. If he suspects that an offence has been committed, he cannot arrest the suspect, but can only require him to stay where he is until the arrival of *la police nationale*. He can search a suspect only by "patting down", and cannot search bags or carry out a body search. In relation to driving offences, however, he can request your driving licence and can carry out a breathalyser test if you have been caught speeding, or have been involved in an accident. If you exceed the speed limit by more than 40 km/h he can seize your vehicle.

Enforcement of fines and penalties

On a UK initiative the EU has now agreed that member states will enforce each others' orders for fines and penalties. This applies not only to motoring offences but to all legal judgments and fines.

Crime

A major problem in some parts of France is theft from occupied vehicles stuck in stationary or slow-moving traffic. The offenders often operate in pairs. They approach a vehicle on a moped. One of them will jump off, open the car door and demand money or valuables, searching the occupants or threatening them with a knife. Once they have recovered enough they then speed off, leaving the unhappy motorist helpless to pursue. Even if the traffic in front starts to move off the offenders will probably have jammed the car door lock so that it will not immediately close, thereby hampering any pursuit. Other motorists are tricked into stopping in the belief that there has been an accident, only to find themselves attacked and robbed. Another tactic, also often carried out with a moped, is to seize a woman's bag, or to cut the straps of the bag.

Trouble with the police and the courts

The UK authorities endeavour to have every arrested person visited by a consular officer within 72 hours.

Accidents and criminal injuries

If you are involved in an accident or have been assaulted you are under a legal obligation to report this to the police. This rule applies even to minor incidents. You should be given a copy of the report to provide to your insurer. There is a system of compensation for those who are assaulted and sustain injury. Note, however, that the system of compensation is not as generous as that in the UK – I understand that the British government pays out more in criminal injuries compensation than all the other governments of the European Union combined.

Tipping

The French do not generally tip, though it is customary to give Christmas boxes (*Les Etrennes*) to the postman, dustman (both around €10), firemen (€15-20, for which you receive a calendar), and 10% of a monthly rental for the concierge in a block of flats.

Consumer Protection

The EU has imposed its own regulations on consumer protection and accordingly French legislation on this is similar to that in other EU states. Your first port of call for any complaint is generally the store or person from which you purchased the goods or service. You should keep all correspondence, including copies of your own letters and ideally make a note of details of any conversation (especially what was said by you and by the seller prior to any purchase) as soon as possible afterwards. A record made a few days, or even weeks or months afterwards is better than no note, as memories generally become less clear over time (and vulnerable to being undermined in any court action that may result).

An extremely useful organisation is the *Union Fédérale de Consommateurs* that publishes *Que Choisir*, rather like Which? in the UK. There is an annual membership fee of €18 for which you receive eleven copies of their regular magazine. *Que Choisir* also produces publications dealing with particular issues. See its web site www.quechoisir.org. Consumer organisations include La Commission de la Sécurité des Consommateurs (CSC), tel: 01 43 19 56 60; www.securiteconso.org. There is an advice line for all administrative and consumer enquiries (Tel: 39 39). The service is available from 8.00 a.m. to 7.00 p.m. Monday to Friday, and 9.00 a.m. to 2.00 p.m. on Saturdays, and costs €0.12 per minute.

The *Code de la Consommation* provides that a *commerçant* has no right to refuse a sale unless he believes that the purchaser cannot pay, or is drunk. They can be fined up to €150. Frauds should be reported to *La Direction Générale de la Concurrence et de la Répression des Fraudes (DGCCCR)* Tel: 0800 202203.

Tradesmen

Tradesmen are supposed to provide quotations (*les devis*) for work costing more than €150. It should set out the price before and after tax, the work to be undertaken and a list of materials. Consumers are not obliged to pay more than the quotation, unless this is covered by a provision in the contract. If you are presented with a higher bill, send the tradesman a *lettre recommandée avec accusé de réception* requesting that the bill be corrected. If the tradesman fails to do this, contact the Direction Départementale de la Concurrence et de la Consommation et de la repression des Fraudes (DDCCRF). For tips on carrying out work yourself see the DIY guide on www.publishingInternet.com (in English).

The black market

Take care when having work carried out at your house. Always ask for proof that the person is properly registered with the social security authorities and has professional insurance, and request sight of his *carte d'identification* issued by the *Chambre de Métiers* – there are a considerable number of British tradesmen who are working in France without complying with French requirements. If they do not have social security cover and have an accident, you might find them arguing that they were employed by you, and seeking to recover the costs of medical treatment. If they cause damage to your property or belongings, and are uninsured, your own insurers may well refuse to pay on the grounds that the workmen should have been carrying their own professional insurance. Whilst engaging someone on the black market may be cheaper, it is not only illegal, but is fraught with problems. If you do prefer to engage someone with whom you can speak in English, consider visiting www.artisan-anglais.com which includes the registration number and other details for each trader, or www.findatradeinfrance.com, where for a modest fee they will recommend a tradesman.

Employing resident domestic staff

Those who employ gardeners, child-minders or other staff should note that these employments are regulated by different *Conventions Collectives* that set out requirements for pay, accommodation, dismissal etc. Any accommodation provided to such employees is part of their remuneration and the law is not the same as that between ordinary landlords and tenants. It is common for the *conventions* to require employers to give three months notice, and the three-month notice period will most probably apply to the accommodation as well.

Remember that if you take on someone to provide part-time or even temporary or irregular help at home, such as a cleaner, gardener or babysitter, you are legally required to notify the authorities and to pay social security contributions. Failure to do so can result is significant fines. The system of *Emploi Service Chèques* was introduced to make it easier for those employing irregular staff to comply with the formalities (and to claim the significant tax relief available). An employer obtains a "cheque book" from his bank or a post-office, completes a form and sends it with his bank details to the Centre National de Traitement de Chèque Emploi Service Social (CNICES). The cheques, which are paid to the employee, also replace the contract of employment, the pay slip and the request for registration with the social security system. Security contributions for the employee are deducted from an employer's bank account by the CNICES. The employer completes the cheques to pay the employee, each time sending a notification to CNICES, which then sends a pay slip to the employee. The advantage of using the system for the employer is that he receives a reduction in his personal tax bill, equal to 50% of the amount paid to the employee. In some circumstances the employer can also obtain an exemption in relation to social charges.

Moving house

There is now a web site that you can inform of your change of address that will pass this information to all other government agencies (www.changement-adresse.gouv.fr), such as the CAF, CPAM, and Assedic.

Chapter Eight

Affairs of family and state

Getting married in France

A marriage ceremony may take place at the *mairie* of either spouse, providing he or she has been resident there continuously for at least a month prior to the date fixed for the marriage. The couple will need to provide the *mairie* with their birth certificates, up to date medical certificates and the names and addresses of two witnesses. Widows are not permitted to remarry until 300 days after the death of their spouse, and a divorced woman may not remarry until 300 days have elapsed since her divorce (though she may make application to the courts for authority to marry earlier).

Newly weds receive a significant bonus from the tax authorities during the year of their marriage. In brief they make three tax declarations in that year. Each person makes a separate tax declaration of their income up to the date of marriage, and they make a joint declaration for the income in the remainder of the tax year after the date of marriage. These three tax declarations are then treated as if submitted by three separate individuals, each with a full year's tax allowance. This significantly reduces the couple's tax bill, often meaning that no tax is payable for the year of marriage. From a tax point of view, the best time to marry is in June or July – the middle of the tax year, assuming that your income remains fairly constant throughout that tax year.

Le régime matrimonial

Where there is no marriage contract, as is the case for 80% of married couples in France, the couple are subject to the *régime de communauté d'acquêts*. Under this system, the salaries, savings, income from letting property, received by either party *during* the marriage become joint property, as do any business or other assets created by either party *during* the marriage, even if held only in one of their names. Partners are also liable for each other debts contracted *during* the marriage. Should one partner be unable (or unwilling) to settle a debt, the creditor can proceed to enforce the debt against joint property. On a divorce, joint assets are subject to a 50% split. On other hand, assets owned by each partner *before* the marriage remain solely their own property, as do assets that they inherit from or are given by their respective families. This *régime* is most suited to salaried employees, where partners' professional activities do not place their spouse at financial risk.

Those running their own businesses, however, are often advised to adopt the regime of *séparation des biens*, which is the closest to the legal position in the England. Here everything is owned separately. Assets bought by one parter in his or her own name remain his own personal property, even if purchased with the other partner's money. The main advantage is that the partners are not liable for each other's debts, and accordingly if one partner's business fails, all those assets belonging to the other partner are protected from the defaulting partner's creditors. This is also the option frequently chosen on a remarriage. Even under this system, it is possible for the couple to chose to elect to hold some assets jointly, such as their home, or a car. Further, debts entered into by either partner to facilate their family life together, or for the education of their children, are debts for which they are both liable. You should also note that many lending establishments now insist that a spouse acts as a guarantor of a proposed loan to their partner to enable them to enforce the loan against either. This clearly reduces the advantage of the regime of *séparation des biens*.

A third option is that of *la participation aux acquêts*. This is a mixture of the two regimes just mentioned, and is often chosen by young couples. During the marriage everything is owned separately, but on dissolution of the marriage each partner is entitled to 50% of the assets or wealth created by their partner during the marriage. This has the advantage of protecting the assets of each of the partners from the other's creditors during the marriage (for example should one partner's business fail), whereas on a divorce a partner shares equally in the benefits of any business created by the other during the marriage.

A fourth option is *la communauté universelle* whereby all assets (and debts) held by the partners both before and after marriage, become their joint property. Under this regime it is possible to insert a clause to enable the surviving spouse to become the sole owner of all the couple's property on the first death. This protects the couple's estate from their children during the surviving spouse's lifetime. No inheritance tax is payable on such a transfer. The main disadvantage of this regime, is where the couple have children or grandchildren and have a sizable estate – more inheritance tax will be payable on the death of the surviving spouse, than would have been payable had some of the assets been passed directly to the children on the death of the first to die. This regime is seldom, if ever, an option where one or other of the couple has children from another relationship as the children have rights against their parent's estate, and could bring proceedings to enforce their rights.

These matrimonial regimes have different consequences for your tax and inheritance position. It is imperative to take advice from a *notaire*, *avocat* or a competent financial adviser. For the most part the British in France continue to opt for separate ownership, but generally holding some property jointly, notably the matrimonial home and a joint bank account.

It is possible to change from one *régime matrimonial* to another, but only after a delay of two years from the date of the marriage, or your last change of regime. You must consult a *notaire* who will prepare the necessary documentation. This must then be submitted by an avocat to the *Tribunal de Grande Instance* where the judge will consider whether the proposed change is in the interests of the family and whether it is an attempt to avoid creditors. The procedure takes six months to a year, and costs around €800 for the notaire and €1,500 for the avocat and court fees.

Should you wish to enter into a pre-marriage contract, you should consult a *notaire* who will give you the necessary documentation to hand to the person responsible for carrying out the civil marriage ceremony. The *notaire's* costs for advising and preparing a marriage contract should be in the region of €400 to €1,500.

Unmarried couples

Living together is often referred to as *union libre, vie maritale or concubinage*. In relation to inheritance and tax affairs the couple are treated as separate individuals, whereas for social security purposes they are considered as if they were married. Each partner spends his income, and deals with his assets as he wishes, and is solely responsible for his own debts, save for debts which are clearly household debts, such as bills for food, or rental for their joint accommodation. It is possible, and often in retrospect highly desirable, to enter into a written contract setting out how the joint household is to be financed, what should happen should the relationship break up and listing the belongings of each at the time when they first begin to live together. Ideally this document should be prepared by a *notaire*. It can also be registered at your local tax office.

Each of the partners has the same rights in relation to most (though not all) social security and family benefits and allowances as if they were married. This also applies to couples of the same sex. Accordingly, if one partner does not work, he or she is nevertheless entitled to social security cover on the basis of his working partner's contributions, and is also entitled to cover from a *mutuelle* or other health insurance policy held by his partner. He or she will need to obtain a *certificat de concubinage* from his local *mairie* (though not all *mairies* will oblige), or some other proof, such as his own sworn declaration. For means-tested benefits and allowance the social security authorities take both partners' circumstances into account, and accordingly a person may cease to be entitled to state benefits once he or she starts to live with a partner. In addition the income support (*revenue minimum d'insertion or RMI*) received by a couple is less than the total they would receive if living separately. Should the couple break up, the non-working partner can remain entitled to social security cover under his previous partner's contributions for a period of up to four years. You must inform your *caisse d'assurance-maladie* so they can reimburse you directly. If you are not employed at the end of the four years, you will be entitled to change to *la couverture maladie universelle* (CMU).

PACS

The *Pacte Civil de Solidarité* was first introduced in 1999. It enables adult couples to enter into a legal contract with each other, with rights and obligations, but which falls short of marriage. Adults of the same sex may also enter into a PACS. To enter into a PACS the partners must be living in the same residence, both aged at least 18 and be unmarried or divorced. To date about 130,000 couples have entered into a PACS, with about 30,000 more PACS being entered each year (compared to 280,000 new marriages).

Those who enter into a PACS are jointly liable for debts entered into by one of them for their life together, such as utility bills, and rental payments. Each partner is otherwise entitled to spend his or her earnings as they wish. On the other hand, unless stated to the contrary in the PACS, all assets bought by either party (including furniture, cars, and even a house or apartment) after signing the PACS, become the joint property in equal shares of both partners. Note that if it is impossible to ascertain the date of purchase it is assumed that it was *after* the date the PACS was entered into, and therefore jointly owned. Accordingly the partners may wish to have inventories drawn up as to who owns what at the date they enter into the PACS. Assets received by one partner by way of gift or inheritance after the date of the PACS, remain the sole property of that partner.

Note that as for married couples, there are significant tax advantages during the tax year in which you enter into a PACS, particularly if you enter into the agreement in the middle of the tax year. Entering into a PACS also gives your partner certain health insurance rights – if one person is covered under the state system, then a partner under a PACS may be entitled to cover as a beneficiary. If they work in the same enterprise, partners are entitled to take holidays at the same time. Partners to a PACS are under an obligation to maintain and support each other in the same way as married partners.

Application for a PACS is made to your local *Tribunal d'Instance*. The court will merely register a PACS, and will not be concerned with the terms contained. You should seriously considering seeking the advice of a *notaire* or *avocat*. If you wish pass any assets to your PACS partner on your death, you will in any event need to make a will. The *notaire's* charges for drawing up a PACS will be in the region of €400 to €1,500 depending on the complexities of your affairs. You can ask him to retain a copy of the PACS for safekeeping, or officially register it, in case your partner should later be unable to locate a copy. It is possible to later change the terms of a PACS. The French have invented a verb that means to enter into a PACS: *pacser*.

Divorce and matrimonial problems

The procedures for divorce have been simplified as from the 1st January 2005. Where both spouses request a divorce and are in agreement about arrangements for their children, and about financial matters, it is now usual to have only one hearing. The judge is able to grant a divorce providing he or she is satisfied that it would not be against the interests of any of the children of the marriage, or against the interest of either spouse. Whereas a divorce, even where the parties were in agreement, used to take around nine months, it can now be completed within three months or so. One spouse can now request a divorce after two years separation, whereas previously the period was six years.

As to a divorce based on fault, this is now limited to the most serious cases, such as those involving matrimonial violence. The couple are now directed towards a mediator in order to encourage agreement. A spouse at fault is no longer penalised when it comes to the financial arrangements arising from the divorce, and indeed can bring a financial claim against the innocent spouse. If the parties cannot reach agreement between themselves then the court will decide. The matters that the courts now take into account are now more similar to those that would be considered by a British court. In a new departure, a spouse can now obtain an injunction excluding a violent partner from the matrimonial home *before* commencing divorce proceedings (rather similar to wider legislation introduced in England and Wales in 1974). The spouse obtaining such an order has three months in which to commence divorce proceedings. Matrimonial violence is a serious problem in France that the authorities are only just beginning to tackle. An estimated two million women are beaten by their husbands, and over seventy women are killed by their husbands or boyfriends each year in France. It is a problem amongst every social class. There are few centres for battered women – information about such facilities can be obtained from *SOS Femmes Accueil* Tel: 03 25065070; www.sosfemmes.com. France has to-date been very remiss about dealing with domestic violence. The first official analysis of the problem was only carried out very recently.

Note that it is no longer possible for one parent to avoid paying UK maintenance payments because he or she is in France, or by moving to France. Similarly a French court order can be implemented in the UK. For enforcement of a UK order in France, the court order should be served on the paying party by a *huissier*. If the maintenance payments in respect of a child remain unpaid for more than two months this could be held to constitute a partial abandonment by the paying parent (*délit d'abandon de famille*). This is a criminal offence for which the parent can receive a prison sentence of up to two years and/or a fine of up to €1,500. Hundreds of fathers in particular can and do go to prison. Generally, however, it is possible to extract the maintenance payments, for example, by a deduction from their salary or from their bank account. Defaulting parents should note that if they have assets or an earning capacity the court system is very likely to catch up with them. The costs incurred in doing this can add substantially to the amounts they have to pay.

For advice on women's rights and children's rights contact your local *Centre d'Information sur les Droits des Femmes et des Familles* (CNIDFF).

Deaths and Burials

Foreign residents dying in France can, of course, be buried or cremated there. The law provides that this must be done within six working days (including Saturdays, but excluding Sundays and Bank Holidays). Advice can be obtained from an undertaker (*société de pompes funèbres*). You will need the deceased's birth certificate (with a translation in French from a certified translator) and the *acte de décès* (the undertaker should arrange this for you). For a cremation, ashes can be scattered in the rest garden of the crematorium. You will need permission to scatter ashes elsewhere. For burials you will need to purchase a plot (*une concession*) for which you should contact the *mairie*. For further details see www.afif.asso.fr (the web site of *L'Association Française d'Information Funéraire*). The web site contains information in English, including on what to do when someone dies at home, and a French / English dictionary of vocabulary that you might need to know. The British Embassy web site (www.amb-grandebretagne.fr) has details of official procedures relating to deaths and burials (go to "English" – "Services for Britons in France" - "Births, Marriages and Deaths"). The information makes it clear that the Foreign and Commonwealth Office are willing to offer help and advice where possible.

Taking French nationality

To apply for French nationality you must be over 18, and must have resided in France continuously for at least five years (or two years for those who have successfully completed at least two years of further education in France). In addition, you must derive your earnings from France, prove that you are able to speak and write French to a reasonable standard, are of good character and are loyal to France. The term "good character" means that you have no criminal conviction punishable with a sentence of imprisonment of six months or more.

Those wishing to apply for citizenship should do so at their local *préfecture*. The procedure takes around 12 months, and will include an assessment of your ability to assimilate into French society. The requirements are more relaxed (and the procedure different) for those who marry a French citizen, or who were born in France.

Before applying to become a French citizen (or indeed a citizen of any country) you should ensure that you are fully aware of both the advantages and the disadvantages. Your country of origin will not be prepared to interfere with any demands made upon you by your adopted country, such as military service, or indeed conscription. According to the Home Office, Her Majesty has no objection to British subjects applying for citizenship of a foreign state or states, without losing their British nationality. If you do decide to take on French nationality, do remember that it comes with no guarantee of having a sense of belonging. Ultimately, having a sense of being *at home* is perhaps the most important element of all.

Voting whilst in France

Non-French EU residents have the right to vote (and stand) in local and European elections. Registration takes place at your local *mairie*. British residents in France who have been registered to vote in the UK within the last 15 years can apply to be overseas voters. For those who were too young to register when they left the UK, they can register as overseas voters if a parent or guardian was registered. Forms and further information on voting in both French and UK elections is to be found at www.aboutmyvote.co.uk. Overseas voters can apply to vote by post or by proxy. They are entitled to vote in national and European elections.

Chapter Nine

EDUCATION

Pre-school education

It is at the pre-school stages that British and foreign parents most often make use of the facilities provided by the French education system. Pre-school education in France is either free or subsidised, making it far less costly than the options provided by the private British or international schools. Moreover, it means that your child has a concentrated exposure to the French language at a time when he is most receptive to learning it. Many parents see this as a significant benefit, though some effort is needed to ensure that a child's level of English develops to a sufficient degree to enable him to progress into a British or international school. A significant number of foreign parents keep their children at French primary schools, and make the move to an English/international education when their child is aged 12.

Choices for pre-school include *crèches* (day nurseries often run by the local authority for children from two months to three years); *halte-garderies* (for children between three months and six years) and placing your child with an *assistante maternelle*. The latter is a registered child minder who looks after one or more children in her home. In many areas there is a shortage of places for pre-school children, and you should make enquiries as early as possible. *Crèches* and *halte-garderies* are listed in the yellow pages (together under *Crèches*). A list of *assistantes maternelles* will be kept by your local *Mairie*, though some are also listed in the Yellow Pages. Parents who place their child with an *assistante maternelle*, in a *crèche* or a *halte-garderie* are entitled to a tax credit equal to 25% of the costs.

Those who employ someone to look after their children at home (*une garde d'enfant*) are now entitled to deduct half the cost of the salary and social security costs associated with employing that person against their own income for tax purposes.

From the age of about four your child can start state nursery school, generally attached to your primary school. This is free. It is divided into three years: *la petite section, la moyenne section* and *la grande section*. You will need proof of vaccinations for diphtheria, tetanus, poliomyelitis and tuberculosis as a condition of school entry.

Options for primary and secondary education

The range of choice is determined very much by where you are living. In Paris, the larger cities, and the French Riviera there are a number of private and state international schools and also British and American schools. There are many French private schools, including a few boarding schools. A high proportion of private schools are Catholic, though non-Catholics are often admitted. Further information on education and schools can be obtained from www.education.gouv.fr (the French Ministry of Education); The English Language Schools Association: 43 rue des Binelles, 92310 Sèvres Tel: 01 45340411; The British Council at www.britishcouncil.for (see the Education Information Service for details of the main English, American and International schools); www.ydelta.free.fr/school.htm; www.angloinfo.com (for schools on the Riviera), and www.asaweb.net/ecoles-chretiennes/adresses.html (for a list of Protestant schools in France, Belgium and Switzerland).

International, British and American private schools

For the most part these are day schools. They are much more expensive than most private French schools, generally costing €10,000 – €12,000 for secondary school, and a little less for primary. They make only small reductions in their fees for a second or subsequent child, and also require a registration fee (often around €600 per child). Most schools demand a full term's notice of leaving, or payment of a term's fees.

The British schools tend to follow the UK curriculum i.e. the National Curriculum tests (though often only internally marked), GCSE O levels and A-levels. In the more international schools pupils take the International Baccalaureate (in English). Extra-curricular activities receive far greater emphasis than in French schools. International schools generally start from nursery age and go all the way through to age 18. A list of international private schools can be found on several websites including www.ecis.org, and www.nabss.org. General guidance can also be obtained from ELSA-France (English Language Schools Association) - see above. Further details for each region are included in Chapter 1.

The international private schools are relatively small in size, in many cases having fewer than 500 pupils. This often results in a convivial atmosphere with friendships being quick to develop. On the other hand, these schools tend to have a rapid turnover of pupils with large numbers leaving each year as their parents move with their jobs. A small school size also means that the choice of subjects available at GCSE and A-level/Baccalaureate is often rather limited. Accordingly, if you have a choice of schools, and your child is likely to remain there during these examination years, it is wise to ascertain not only which subjects are taught in the school, but also which subjects can be studied together – the school may not be able to offer certain combinations, owing to practical difficulties of time tabling and staffing.

It is not easy as a parent to evaluate the standard of education provided by theses international private schools, including those that follow the British curriculum. They have large numbers of pupils whose first language is not English or indeed French. Whilst your child is exposed to the benefits of an education in a multi-cultural environment, if a large number of his class mates are having to follow lessons in a language which is not their own (and in some cases this can apply to well over half the class), this will inevitably slow down the class as a whole to some degree. Some schools approach this problem by streaming, but as most of the private schools are not particularly large there is a limit on the extent to which they can do this. There are a number of state international schools in France (see below for details) covering both primary and secondary level education.

Private French schools

These fall into two categories – those that are assisted by the state (*sous-contrat*), such as many of the Catholic schools, and those that are not. *Sous-contrat* schools are independent of the state, but have the salaries of their teaching staff financed from state funds. Parents, including non-Catholics, often elect to send their children to Catholic schools because they tend to provide a more protected environment for their children, and educational standards tend to be higher than in state schools. There are a handful of private protestant schools in France (see www.huguenots.net), a number of boarding schools, and some schools that purport to be bilingual. Details of local private schools are to be found in *Les Pages Jaunes* under *Enseignement primaire: écoles privées* and *Enseignement secondaires: collèges privés*. I know of at least one Catholic school that in the last two years has opened an *anglophone* section for English speakers, rather similar to those that have existed in the public sector for some time (see below). A major advantage of sending your child to a private school is that he or she does not have to change schools if you move house, for example if you rent initially and only buy after living in the area for 12 months or so.

Further information about French private schools is available from *Le Centre Nationale de Documentation sur l'Enseignement Privé*, 20, rue Faubert, 75007 (01 47053268). For further details see the site www.fabert.com

Public International Schools

There are a number of French state primary schools, and secondary schools (*such as the Centre International de Valbonne* on the *Côte d'Azur*) that have for some time had an *anglophone section* in which a child carries out part of his studies in French and part in English. The long-term aim is for pupils to take the International Baccalaureate at age 18. These schools are relatively inexpensive for the primary years and for the years at *college* (around €2,000 per year), though the costs can rise steeply thereafter. For further information see www.ydelta.free.fr/school.htm, and also the information for each region in Chapter 1.

French state school

Education in state school is free, though parents are responsible for the cost of books, and school materials such as exercise books, pens, pencils, crayons and so on, as well as for the cost of extra-curricular activities. If your child is to attend state school, it must be within a certain distance of your home. This will normally mean the nearest school, but in some circumstances it is possible to be admitted to another school. Accordingly, it would be wise to make enquiries about the local school, and indeed see if the headteacher is willing to meet you, *before* you chose your home. Application for state schools is generally via your local *mairie*. Standards at state schools can vary widely. In some areas, for example in Finistère in Brittany, the local authorities have provided extra teaching staff to assist English children who have moved into their area.

The French school system

I have often heard adverse comparisons made between the British and French education systems, to the detriment of our own. In a good many cases the commentator is simply uninformed, and the picture is in fact rather more complicated than is suggested. In attempting to make any comparison it is important firstly to realise that the two systems are very different indeed, secondly that they are both in a state of change (notably on the UK side with the introduction of SATS), and thirdly that many French people are not at all happy with their own system.

One disadvantage that faces the French education system is the fact that the French language is much more complicated than English, and in primary schools a greater amount of time is spent by French children mastering their language, than is spent by English primary school children learning English. Accordingly less time is devoted to other subjects, primarily Maths. A further problem is that French schools place a heavy emphasis on learning the technical rules of grammar. Whilst grammatical tools are an essential part of a language, they are only tools to achieving a greater goal (an ability to express oneself orally and in writing, and to understand others) and they are not a goal in themselves. Whilst a detailed knowledge of these rules may be very useful for the study of

French or a foreign language at university level, the study of them makes for a pretty dry education at primary level! Indeed, the French adopt the same highly grammatical approach to the study of English during secondary school. This perhaps explains why so many of them dislike the language, and so few are good at it. According to a recent report by the OECD French school pupils were slightly ahead at age 15 compared to the average pupil across the 41 countries covered by the report. In Mathematics the French students ranked 13th amongst the 41 countries studied. In modern languages, however, the French themselves recognise that much improvement is required.

In France schools are mixed. There is no uniform. There tends to be less of a school identity or team spirit, with sport, drama and music playing a relatively small role in school life. Inter-school competitions are far less common than in the UK.

The French are rather more flexible than the British about what age a child can start primary school, and you will find that there is a wider age range of children in each year than in the UK, with some children starting earlier and some later than "*the norm*". The French also operate a system of *redoublement* whereby if a child is in difficulties he or she will be required to repeat the previous year's schooling. Whilst *redoubling* a child sounds logical and can work in some cases, it has major drawbacks. Firstly a child loses the friends that it has made in its current year group, secondly it continues its education with children who are on average a year younger than would otherwise be the case (which can be a problem if a child was already old for its year) and thirdly the child carries the label of being a *redoublant* and can be the subject of taunting etc. Frequently a child who is put back a year simply exchanges the bottom place of the class he was in for the bottom place of the class in a year below and is a lot unhappier as a result.

The school day generally starts at 08.00 or 08.15 with nearly a two-hour break for lunch at around 11.30. There is little in the way of organised activities during this time. School ends at around 16.00 in primary school, and at 16.30 in secondary school. Whilst at first glance it appears that French children spend longer at school than their British counterparts, in practice this is not the case. France has significantly more bank holidays than the UK, many of which fall in term time, the summer term often finishes before the end of June, school trips normally take place during the school term (not during the holidays as in the UK) and in the primary school several half days a year are devoted to teacher training, during which children are not taught and for which you will often have to make your own arrangements.

The school year begins in early September, usually slightly later than in the UK. *La rentrée des classes* is a hectic time for parents who are provided with often quite a long list of items to purchase, such as several different types of exercise books and a range of items for a child's pencil case(s). If you wish to avoid the mad frenzy in the supermarkets you could pass your list to your local *papeterie*. Whilst their prices are somewhat higher than the supermarket they will often give you a discount on their normal prices, and save you considerable time and effort. There is a means tested grant of about €250 per child that is currently claimed by around three million families. For further details contact your *caisse d'allocations familiales*.

From 2005, as part of its campaign to counter the increasing levels of obesity amongst school children the government imposed a ban on the sale in schools of sugared drinks via automatic vending machines. For the moment the ban does not extend to chocolates and sweets.

Primary schools (*écoles primaires*, ages 6 to 11)

In primary school the emphasis is on learning the French language, including its complex rules of grammar, and memorising and reciting French poetry. Less time is spent on Maths than in the UK. The curriculum includes sport and English from year 4 (CM1). The law forbids a primary school teacher (referred to as *maître or maîtresse*) from giving written homework. The years at primary school are divided into three cycles:

Year 1: CP (*Cours Préparatoire*)
Years 2 & 3: CE 1 and CE2 (*Cours Elémentaires*)
Years 4 & 5: CM1 and CM2 (*Cours Moyens*)

If a child does not satisfactorily complete a cycle then he may be required to repeat the last year of that cycle again (see above for a discussion of the system of *redoublement*). At the beginning of CE2 your child will sit a national test. This is a "low key" test about which you will be told little or nothing. Schools do not appear to prepare pupils specifically for this test, though the result will be kept with your child's school records.

Some primary schools still have a half-day on Wednesday (finishing at around 11.15 a.m.), though others have decided against any school on Wednesday and have slightly longer school terms. Various activities are arranged by local *mairies* to occupy children on Wednesdays.

Secondary schools (*collège, age 11-16*)

The transition to *collège* from primary school is obviously a major landmark in a child's life. It will often involve a move from the environment of a small school, to a much larger establishment with many more pupils. From an academic perspective, however, the first year at *collège* (*sixième*) should not be traumatic. The objective over the first two terms is simply to assess your child's ability and to ensure that he has a thorough understanding of the main concepts that he should have grasped during his years at primary school. It will only be during the short third term that your child will begin to move on to new ground.

Collège is divided into three cycles:

6 *ième* (1st year)   - *observation et orientation*

5 *ième* & 4 ième(2nd & 3rd years)- *cycle central*

3 *ième* (4th year)   - *orientation*

If a child does not satisfactorily complete a cycle, then it can be required to repeat the last year of that cycle (see above for a discussion of *redoublement*). The last year of *collège* (i.e. 3 *ième*) is concerned with deciding the direction in which your child will continue his studies, in particular whether he will move onto an academic education or pursue a non-academic more vocational training course. At the end of 3 ième each child sits state examinations called *le brevet*.

Whilst academically the transition from primary school to *collège* is fairly gentle, in other respects there are major changes. In primary school, in my opinion, there is a tendency to still "baby" children even in the last two years. When they arrive in *collège*, however, they are suddenly treated as adolescents (*ados*), and are given far more freedom about their use of time than in an English school. A significant difference is that in French schools it is normal for children to have *les trous* (holes) in their school day covering several hours a week. Your child will generally start school at 8.00 a.m. (though on some days it could be later), but might for example, stop classes at 11.00 a.m. and have no further classes until perhaps 3.30 p.m. In the interval your child is expected to attend the school library (*Le Centre de Documentation et d'Information – Le CDI*), or to go *en permanence* (or *perm*, for short). The latter consists of attending a large room under the surveillance of often a non-teaching member of staff. Your child may need to book itself in advance to the library if it wishes to avoid *les heures de perm*. Parents often arrange for their child to go home during these holes in their school day, but obviously this can be difficult to organise. The government has promised to reduce the incidence of these holes. Whilst your child may leave school at a set time of 16.00 or 16.30 most days a week, it is quite possible that one day a week lessons will not finish until 17.00 or even later.

At the beginning of *sixième* parents are asked to attend a meeting (*une réunion*) at the school at which the programme for *sixième* and life in *collège* is explained. Each parent should also receive a guide published by the *Office National d'Information sur les Enseignements et les Professions (ONISEP)* entitled *L'entrée en 6e – le guide des parents*. It is available for purchase at other times at a cost of €3.50. ONISEP also produces a series of career guides (see its web site at www.onisep.fr or tel: 01 64 80 38 00).

Students at *collège* receive 25 hours of tuition per week, with the emphasis on French, Maths, and the study of a foreign language (usually English), with relatively little emphasis on science subjects at this stage. Your child will be given a *carnet de liaison* or *carnet de correspondance*. This sets out the school rules, will contain your child's school timetable, and a record of whether or not you have given your child permission to leave the school premises. It also contains a note of any reprimands or punishments your child receives, and serves as a means of communication between you and the school.

At the beginning of *sixième* your child will undergo tests (*évaluations*) in Mathematics and French, rather similar to those taken at the beginning of CE2 in primary school. Again pupils are generally given no preparation for these tests. They are not particularly demanding, and appear designed to identify the weakest children who may then be given extra help in these subjects. At the end of each term you will be sent *un bulletin scolaire*.

One aspect of school life that is rather different from that in the UK is the *Conseils de Classe* that meet at the end of each term. They are attended not only by teaching staff, but also by two elected representatives from among parents at the school (generally not the parents of children in your child's class) and by two elected representatives from the class (*les délégués de classe*). The *Conseil de Classe* discusses each child's progress during the term. If a child has problems, then the discussion can include matters relating to his conduct, his health, or family circumstances. All those participating in the *conseil*, including the two parents and two pupils, have a duty not to divulge to others information that they learn about other pupils at the *conseil*. Accordingly, whilst French law requires doctors and lawyers to keep confidences closely guarded, once confidential information moves into the school arena, it can be shared with two parents from the school, and two of your child's classmates! Indeed the class representative is supposed to be your child's representative at the *Conseil de Classe*, and so may seek to discuss any problems with your child. The pupil and parent representatives are re-elected each year, and accordingly frequently change from year to year.

Parents can contact teaching staff to discuss a child's progress. More general questions should be addressed to your child's class teacher (*le professeur principal*).

Lycée (16-18)

After completing the brevet children move on to study for the *baccalauréat* or *le bac* over a period of three years (2ième, *première and terminale*.) There are various forms of bac including a science bac, a literary bac, a general bac and more vocational bacs. All the non-vocational courses include the same basic core subjects, including Maths, French and a foreign language, though studied in different depths. Some *lycées* form part of the same establishment as a *collège*, whereas others are completely separate.

Bilingual children

A child's ability to learn a foreign language is obviously greatest in its early years, i.e. before the age of six. If you place your child in a British, American or private international school it is extremely unlikely that he will acquire a high level of French, certainly not without a lot more input. On the other hand if your child attends French school from an early age then fluency in French is likely to be guaranteed. The problem here is that most English children who go through the French school system fail to acquire, or simply lose, fluency in English. Attractive though it may be to have a child who speaks fluent French, it seems absurd to gain this at the expense of losing the world's main language. Whilst it is possible for your child to acquire and retain fluency in both languages, this is only with determined and continuous effort on the child's part, and especially on the part of its parents.

The different educational year groups
for France and the UK

Nursery (2-3) *Maternelle (Petite Section & Moyenne Section)*
Year 1 Infants (5-6) *Maternelle, Grande Section*

Ecole Primaire

Year 2 (6-7)	*CP*
Year 3 (7-8)	*CE1*
Year 4 (8-9)	*CE2*
Year 5 (9-10)	*CM1*
Year 6 (10-11)	*CM2*
Collège	
Year 7 (11-12)	*6ième*
Year 8 (12-13)	*5ième*
Year 9 (13-14)	*4ième*
Year 10 (14-15)	*3ième*
Lycée	
Year 11 (15-16)	*2ième*
Year 12 (16-17)	*Première*
Year 13 (17-18)	*Terminale*

University education

There is a good selection of universities in France, including several Catholic and private universities. Whilst fees are low for both French and EU nationals, the facilities are stretched to capacity. There is little in the way of extra-curricular activities, in contrast to the UK. Applications are made in January, with the academic year starting in September. Foreign students will be required to undergo a language aptitude test. Students can obtain guidance in relation to working to financing their studies from a new publication by the *Union Internationale des Etudiants de France*. For details see www.unef.fr or write to UNEF, 112 boulevard de la Villette 75019 Paris. Many students in France chose to live at home in order to save on accommodation expenses. Following the completion of the first two years of university study students receive the *Diplôme d'Etudes Universitaires Générales* or *DEUG*. Thereafter studies are more specialised. On completion of a third year a *Licence* is awarded which equates to a BA or BSc. The *Maîtrise* equates to the Master of Arts or Master of Science qualification.

There is also the possibility of foreign students enrolling in a French university as a visiting student for up to one academic year, although you cannot count these studies towards a degree in France should you later wish to continue your studies in France (see also under the Erasmus programme, below). You can obtain information from the *Vicerrectorado de Alumnos* or the International Relations office at your university.

Some of the more select establishments of higher education, such as *Les Grandes Ecoles* (covering public service, commerce, industry and politics) have been severely criticised for their selection criteria, with the vast majority of their entrants being from middle class backgrounds. In 2003 Sciences-Po introduced special competitive entrance requirements for applicants coming from *lycées* in deprived areas. 2005 saw the launch of a government charter aimed at opening up other such institutions. The normal path to acceptances at a *grande école* is a high result at the *baccalauréat* followed by up to two years of additional study prior to further examinations.

English speakers, just like French nationals, are entitled to a grant from CROUS, a body responsible for funding studies in the UK. Information on UK universities can be conveniently accessed via www.sundaytimes.co.uk/universityguide. Those considering a year out should consult www.gapyear.com and www.yearoutgroup.org:

The Open University

Study with the Open University is perfectly possible in France. You are unlikely to have many face-to-face tutorials (telephone tutorials are arranged instead) and the cost is substantially higher. However, if you (or your spouse) pay income tax in the UK, you should normally only have to pay the UK rate for Open University courses. Information about the Open University's courses, and the Open University Business School can be found on their respective websites: www.open.ac.uk and www.oubs.open.ac.uk

European educational and training programmes

The European Commission is keen to promote cross-border educational programmes in order to foster the European identity, and the growth of intra-EU exchanges of ideas and information. The most well known programme is the Erasmus Programme that provides students with a 3-12 month stay at a university or other higher education institution of another European country. The student, his home institution and the host institution sign up to a Learning Agreement. Whilst they are abroad students must undergo the examinations set by the host institution, which may include written and/or oral examination in the language of the host institution. The examination should be recognised by the student's home institution. It is possible to incorporate a work placement during a period on the Erasmus Programme.

Students generally receive additional financial assistance to help with travel costs and higher costs of living. The European Commission may also fund language tuition for the student before beginning the programme. Several hundred thousand students have taken part in the Erasmus Programme and most European universities participate in the scheme, as do some other higher educational institutions. For further information see the EU's Gateway to Europe, accessible via www.europe.eu.int and www.europe.eu.int/ploteus.

Information on educational and training opportunties in Europe can be accessed via the European Commission's service known as PLOTEUS (Portal on Learning Opportunities Throughout Europe). The website, www.europa.eu.int/ploteus, includes details of national education and training systems, European exchange of programmes and grants, as well as details of other sources for information. Guidance can also be obtained from the Euroguide Network (see www.euroguidance.org.uk).

Qualifications equivalence

Information on equivalence of educational qualifications can be obtained from one of the network of National Academic Recognition Information Centres (NARICs). See the website: http://www.enic-naric.net

Chapter Ten

HEALTHCARE AND THE FRENCH HEALTH SYSTEM

The almost unanimous view amongst British residents in France is that the standard of health care in France is much higher than in the UK. This is supported by official studies, such as that carried out by the World Health Organisation that ranked France first in the quality of health care. France spends more on health, has far more doctors and pharmacies per head of population and has a higher life expectancy than the UK. Generally you can obtain an initial appointment with a consultant, and any necessary treatment more quickly than in the UK.

Over the past few years, however, the system has shown signs of severe strain. The French use medical services intensively. The level of prescriptions of drugs, including in many cases the unnecessary and even pointless prescription of antibiotics, is extraordinarily high, with the French taking more medication than the residents of any other nation in Europe. The government is taking serious measures to reduce its drugs bill, including steps to increase the proportion of drugs that are generic (presently not much above 15% – far less than in the UK). A major factor in the health and drugs bill is the preoccupation the French have with *le stress*. According to a recent survey a third of the French have taken medication "for their nerves", up to 15% have undergone some form of psychotherapy, 30% claimed to have some psychological difficulty at the time of the study, and 11% claimed to have had suffered from serious depression in the two weeks prior to the study. The problem is most severe amongst the divorced, the unemployed and those on low incomes. A common treatment for stress is to attend a thalassotherapy centre (i.e. sea water therapy), which is currently reimbursable. When I suggested to a French friend that this was nothing short of a holiday on the state he became somewhat agitated!

The truth is that the health budget has got out of control. The government has already taken some major steps, although to what extent some of these will reduce the financial shortfall is questionable. Further measures are likely to be needed in the near future.

Le Médecin Traitant

A major change for French patients has been the introduction of the idea of registration with a particular doctor. As from 1st July 2005 French residents were supposed to register with a *médecin traitant*, reminiscent of the UK family doctor. The aim of this reform is to reduce the cost of excessive treatment. Under these new rules, if a patient wishes to see a consultant, he must pass via his *médecin traitant* who is now the first port of call for patients and is supposed to co-ordinate the patient's healthcare. A patient is not obliged to appoint a general practitioner (*médecin généraliste*) as his *médecin traitant* although this will be the choice of most patients. One could, for example, appoint a consultant from whom one is receiving care for a long-term illness. Parents are not obliged to appoint a *médecin traitant* for children under 16, but those aged 16-18 must do so. This need not be the same doctor as that chosen by either of his or her parents, though one of the child's parents must consent to the choice of doctor. A student must chose a doctor either in his home town, or his place of study, but will not be penalised in relation to reimbursement for consulting a different doctor when it is impracticable to consult his *médecin traitant*. Reimbursement is generally limited to a consultation with one consultant only, with the patient having to pay for consultations with other experts. In principle, whilst it is for the *médecin traitant* to decide which type of specialist the patient should consult, the choice of which individual specialist to consult remains the patient's. You can obtain the relevant form for registering with a doctor at www.ameli.fr (click on *Le formulaire de déclaration du médecin traitant*). There is also a help line tel: 0820 77 33 33 (Mon – Fri 8.00 a.m. to 8.00 p.m.)

Patients are not obliged to appoint a *médecin traitant* but if they fail to do so will receive a lower level of reimbursement. This does not apply to consultations whilst on holiday, whilst travelling for work purposes, or in a medical emergency when a patient will receive the normal level of reimbursement. Similar you do not have to pass via a *médecin traitant* to consult a dentist, an ophthalmologist or a gynaecologist.

Patients are free to change their *médecin traitant*, but must obtain the consent of their new doctor, and inform both the *caisse d'assurance maladie* and their existing doctor. A doctor is entitled to refuse to accept a patient's request to be appointed his *médecin traitant*, and is under no obligation to justify or give reasons for his refusal. In many cases doctors may simply not wish to further overburden their lists. This right of refusal could cause substantial problems for patients in rural areas who will not be "fully" reimbursed if they cannot find a *médecin traitant*. Patients refused onto a doctor's list should consult their *caisse primaire d'assurance* that is charged with finding a doctor in such circumstances. Doctors are unhappy at the present arrangements, not least because a *médecin traitant* receives no extra remuneration for his added responsibilities.

Care in the community for the old and the infirm

The French system is poor in its provision of nursing care, and help to patients in the community, particularly the aged. Even in the private sector, there are, for example, relatively few retirement and convalescent homes, or homes for the terminally ill. Britons, and other foreign residents, who are no longer able to manage alone, often find themselves having to return home. France also lags considerably behind other western European countries in its provision of facilities, including access, for the disabled.

Maternity care

The French medical profession take a very "medicalised" approach to childbirth, and expectant mothers are likely to find less freedom of choice here than in the UK. Ideas such as birth plans (though frequently overridden in the UK) are unfamiliar to French doctors and patients. Postnatal follow-up is more limited than in the UK, with no equivalent service to that provided by the community midwife. There are some British midwives who have now set up in France (such as Vivienne Rion, based in the Var). Once a woman knows that she is expecting a baby she should obtain a *carnet de maternité* in which the progress of the pregnancy will be recorded, and in which useful information is set out.

Child care

Parents are given a *carnet de santé* for each child. This is kept by the parent and contains information about child development. It should be taken to each medical appointment when details of treatment, vaccinations etc should be recorded. Your child will also be occasionally seen by medical professionals whilst at school, including for hearing and sight tests. You should be given advance notice of this, and have the option to attend.

Hospital care

Standards in hospitals in France are high. If a parent wishes to stay overnight with a child then rooms are available (*les chambres mère-enfant*) at a cost, including meals, of around €45. As in the UK, hospitals are not the safe havens that many would like to believe. Patients, especially children, are always at risk of mistreatment, whether it be by intruders breaching often inadequate security, other child and adult patients, or indeed in some cases medical staff.

One aspect that you may need to guard against is unnecessary prolonged hospital admissions. A number of France's very good hospitals are charitable private institutions, but are funded by the state social security system. How much they are paid by the state depends upon the amount of care they provide, including in terms of hospital rooms. I have heard of one case where a patient was required to attend a hospital for tests as an outpatient. The person was allocated a hospital room for a whole day, when in fact the tests required attendance at hospital for a much shorter time, and it was questionable whether a room was required at all. Each year the magazine *Le Point* produces an issue devoted to hospitals in France, highlighting the hospitals considered to the best in each speciality.

Preventative health care

The flu vaccine is widely available in France, and is provided free to those over 65, and those suffering from respiratory problems and diabetes. There is an established programme for breast screening (for further information see www.rendezvoussanteplus.net). In order to counter growing levels of obesity, there is now a ban on machines in schools that dispense soft drinks (though chocolate vending-machines are still permitted).

User-friendly doctors

Whilst most doctors in France share a certain arrogance with their UK colleagues, the service they provide is generally more user friendly than in the UK. This may be in part because they are far more numerous (about twice as many per head of population as in the UK), and hence feel a greater need to respond to patient's wishes in order to encourage patients to return to them. Indeed, the government has recently campaigned to reduce the amount of unnecessary and pointless prescriptions of antibiotics, which appears to have been taking place to satisfy a conviction on the part of many patients that they have not received proper treatment if they do not come away from an appointment armed with a prescription.

Despite the introduction of *le médecin traitant* the French system still has a number of advantages over its British counterpart. For women, for example, there are far more female consultants in France. For children, care is more specialised, in that save in rural areas, most are seen by a paediatrican for routine appointments, rather than a GP, there being no requirement to first obtain a referral from the child's *médecin traitant*. Many consultants have surgeries in the high street, as do radiographers. It is generally possible to have a consultation, or have an X-ray taken, without spending hours waiting in a queue, as is often the case in NHS hospitals. Doctors, including hospital doctors, are normally far more prepared to answer a question over the telephone that you may have forgotten to ask at a consultation, though it is of course best to check with his or her secretary when the person is best able to take a call.

Pharmacies

As in many other countries pharmacies have a green neon light outside their premises. There is also a system of duty-chemists open 24 hours a day, seven days a week. The address of the duty out-of-hours pharmacist is posted in the windows of pharmacies, and can also be found in the local newspaper. If you attend hospital and are not kept in, but are given a drugs prescription, you will probably not be able to obtain the medication at the hospital and will have to find a chemist. If you need to do this out of hours it is likely that you will have to go to the nearest 24 hours a day manned police station. As a security measure for the pharmacist they will telephone him or her to let you know that you are coming.

Emergency telephone numbers

SAMU (*Service d'Aide Médicale Urgence*) 15
Police   17
Fire   18

Language difficulties

Like many of the French, French doctors often claim they speak English, when quite frankly they speak hardly any, and certainly not enough to conduct a medical consultation. British consulates keep a list of the doctors in their area known to speak English, and private health insurers and travel associations often keep lists. The websites of the local English-speaking press are often good sources of information on doctors.

Your rights to medical cover and treatment in France

In 2005 the E111 (formerly obtained from a post office to cover you for emergency treatment whilst on a short term visit to another EU country) is being phased out, in favour of a new European health insurance card called an EH1C. This is known in France as the *Carte européene d'assurance maladie* (CEAM). This will also replace the E110, the E119 and the E128. The aim of the change is to facilitate labour mobility within the EU. It is intended that by 2008 the card's chip will include a range of electronic data. In France the CEAM is obtainable from your local *Caisse d'assurance*, in the UK it is envisaged that the card will be available from local post offices. The new card permits holders not only to emergency treatment, but also *necessary routine medical treatment* for a temporary period of up to 12 months spent in another EU country. Holders of the

CEAM will still be required to pay for medical treatment, but are entitled to recover most of the cost when they return to the UK. You will be left with having paid a modest contribution, as you would if you were living and working in France.

Those intending to retire to France, should contact The Pension Service's International Pension Centre, which is part of the Department for Work and Pensions at Newcastle Upon Tyne NE98 1BA (tel: 0191 218 7777) and request copies of the guidance leaflets available. Those receiving a UK state pension have a right to free health care in France and should be provided with an E121 by the UK authorities. This should then be registered with the local *caisse primaire d'assurance maladie*.

If you work in France you will normally be obliged to participate in the French social security system. Employers must register all new employees with the social security authorities and deduct social security contributions from your salary. Health cover (*Couverture Maladie Universelle*, or CMU) is available without charge to residents of France with a household income of less than €6,965 per year. Those with higher incomes pay 8% of declared income, though the calculation is not straightforward, particularly for the self-employed. For further details see www.ameli.fr

If you are a UK national and have been sent to work in France by your employer on a temporary basis, you should be entitled to cover under the French health system while still paying your contributions to the UK system. You will need to obtain Form E106. Once you have received your form back from the UK authorities you should take it to your local *caisse primaire d'assurance maladie* and ask them to record details of your dependants on the form. Contact *Le Service Relations Internationales* to obtain your *Carte Vitale* (see below). People who live and work in UK, but whose families are resident in France, will need to obtain Form E109.

La Carte Vitale

Issued to all residents over 16, this electronic card contains details relating to your health rights, including your name, address and social security number. You will need to produce this whenever you visit a medical professional or obtain medication on prescription. Whilst you are still required to pay for medical services and medication, the *carte vitale* ensures that you are reimbursed within five days directly into your bank account, with no forms to complete. Work is currently in progress to produce computerised files for all patients, with the aim of providing the patient and medical personnel with a complete medical history. Access to these files will be controlled by the patient, but failure to allow a doctor access to your medical files will mean a lower level of reimbursement.

Rates of reimbursement – medical consultations

Consultations are reimbursed at 70% of the standard rate fee. For a consultation with a general practitioner *médecin traitant* you will be charged €20, of which €13 is reimbursed (i.e. 70% less the new €1 *de participation forfaitaire*) by the *sécurité sociale*. A consultation with a consultant will normally cost you about €25, of which €16.50 is reimbursed. If you opt for a private consultation (for example in order to obtain an earlier appointment, or one at a more convenient time, or an appointment with the head of the department), then the doctor is entitled to fix his own level of fee. €60 would not be uncommon. Assuming that this is a referral from your *médecin traitant* or a follow-up appointment you will still be entitled to reimbursement of €16.50, with the final cost to you of the appointment being €43.50 i.e. around £30 and rather less than a private appointment would cost in the UK. Obviously if you have a *mutuelle*, then the final cost to you is reduced further.

Note that rates of reimbursement in relation to dental care are far lower than for other medical care, even in relation to orthodontic care for children.

Rates of reimbursement – hospital care

The French social security system takes direct responsibility for 100% of hospital bills, and you are not required to pay first and wait for reimbursement. This covers surgery, treatment for long-term illness, antenatal care and childbirth. It is for this reason that some people do not have a *mutuelle*, as the cover that is required generally only relates to the fairly modest amount of consultation fees not met by the state system, and some people prefer to simply pay these themselves. On the other hand the rate of reimbursement for post-operative outpatient care has recently been cut to only 65%, which may cause many to reconsider taking out a *mutuelle*. Patients in hospital are required to pay a *forfait journalier*, currently €14, for meals.

Private insurance

A number of French and foreign companies offer health insurance cover (e.g. Exclusive Health Care). Policies vary considerably in the cover provided, in particular in the degree of choice of doctors and hospitals and on matters that are excluded from cover. If you are resident in France, and hence subject to compulsory participation in the French social security system, you may wish to take out a *mutuelle*. This is a policy that covers all or a proportion of those costs not met by the French social security system.

Chapter Eleven

YOU AND YOUR CAR

Importing your car

TVA (VAT) is not payable on bringing a car into France that has been in your ownership for six months or more. You have three months to register the vehicle in France. To do this you must first obtain a *certificat* from your local *Inspecteur de Mines* (ask your local *préfecture* for the address). This will only be granted if your vehicle meets French safety specifications. This is almost invariably straightforward, though you will need to have the headlights of your right hand drive vehicle adjusted.

Once you have the certificate issued by the *Inspecteur de Mines*, you take this to the branch of your local *préfecture* that processes car registrations, together with your passport, your existing car registration document, insurance certificate, and MOT. The authorities will usually there and then provide you with a French registration number and registration document (*la carte grise*). You must then have your new plates fitted (in many cases there will be a supplier within a short distance of the centre). You must then return your UK registration documents to the DVLA, from whom you should obtain a Certificate of Permanent Export (V561).

Car Insurance

Car insurance is more expensive than in the UK, and it is advisable to obtain several quotes. If you are using your foreign-registered car in France, you should check whether the policy covers you for driving in Europe. If not, you will need to ask your insurance company to extend your cover by issuing you with a "Green Card". Those with French-registered vehicles generally take out a policy in France. There are a number of differences between the regulations in the UK and France governing motor insurance. Ensure that you fully understand the extent of the cover under any policy you are contemplating taking out. Take care also to comply with the conditions contained in the policy, including the time limits and other provisions for the reporting of claims. Insurance is considerably cheaper if you have a higher excess. Third party insurance is compulsory. Ensure that you have sufficient third party cover (this needs to be high in case a third party or parties were to suffer serious personal injuries). You can use your foreign non-claims bonus in France, on production of a letter or other written proof from your previous/existing insurers.

If you wish your children to be able to drive, you need to check with your insurers as to whether an additional premium is payable. This will depend partly on whether your child is a regular driver (*habituel*) or only drives occasionally (*occasionel*), and whether your child is male or female. Most insurance companies cover the occasional driving of daughters without additional charge, though make a charge of around €180 to cover a son as an occasional driver. If your son drives your car without the insurer being aware and has an accident, there is a very real risk of your insurance being declared invalid.

Always ensure that you have a *Constat Amiable* in your vehicle as you will need this in the event of an accident. It is a document in duplicate that is completed and signed by both drivers. You can obtain copies in English. It is important to answer the questions and fill in the boxes correctly. It will be almost impossible to go back on the information that you have put down. You must send your copy to your insurers within five working days (the time limit is 48 hours in the case of a theft). Your insurance agency should then contact you to arrange for the vehicle to be examined by an *expert*. This inspection can generally be carried out at the garage where you wish the repairs to be undertaken. The expert will decide what damage should be repaired as a result of the accident, and the cost of doing this. Your insurers will then send the garage an authority to carry out the work, and they will pay the bill. You can arrange for the garage to carry out the work immediately after the expert's inspection so that you do not have to part with your vehicle twice. Often a courtesy car (*véhicule de prêt*) will be provided free of charge (for example if you are having bodywork carried out), and for a modest fee at other times. Given the high cost of taking a taxi, this is usually well worthwhile.

If you have an accident, and the other driver is at fault but uninsured, you should still receive compensation thanks to the *fonds de garantie automobile* that is funded from a 0.1% levy on all insurance premiums.

Purchasing and maintaining a car

The cost of buying a car in France still compares favourably to the UK. Furthermore, with lower interest rates, the cost of financing the purchase of a car is also less. All cars that are more than four years old must be subjected to a *contrôle technique*, similar to the annual MOT in the UK. The first test should take place *before* the car is four years old. Failure to carry out the test in time could result in a fine. Subsequent tests are carried out every two years. The 133-point test must be completed at a certified centre. There is a fee payable of about €40-60 (see the Yellow Pages under *Contrôle Technique* for details of your local centres). Should your car not pass the test you are given two months to carry out the necessary work, after which you can have a re-test usually without a further fee. If you do not have the work completed within that time your vehicle will have to be completely retested. A *contrôle technique* is also obligatory if you sell your vehicle, unless a test has been carried out in the preceding six months. The test centre will mark your *carte grise* to state that the test has been carried out and give you a *macaron* (small sticker) that goes on your windscreen and which states the time limit for the next test. For further information see the detailed information in the section under *Contrôle Technique* in *Les Pages Jaunes*, including the requirements involved in *le check-up*.

Driving Licences and driving tests

A UK issued driving licence is sufficient to enable you to drive in France (EU Directive R123-E/97), but note that in France only those over 18 are permitted to drive, and accordingly it is illegal for a 17 year old with a UK licence to drive in France. Remember also that a UK licence expires when the holder reaches 70, and an application for a new French licence should be made. Ideally leave about two months prior to the expiry of your existing licence.

Your UK licence will not of course contain your current address, as it cannot be amended to show a foreign address. This can cause problems if you are required to produce the licence as ID or are stopped by the police. The solution is to obtain an *enregistrement d'un permis de conduire de l'Union Européen* (F45) from your local *préfecture*. This is free of charge. The F45 shows your current address and should be stapled to your UK licence.

If you lose your driving licence you should report the loss as soon as possible to the *gendarmerie*. Apart from anything else, drivers face a fine of €38 if they cannot produce a licence when requested to do so. You should be given a *récépissé* as proof that you have reported the loss, and you can produce this if stopped by the police. You must then apply for a new licence from your local *Préfecture*, or *Sous-Préfecture* where you will be asked to produce the receipt from the police, your passport and three recent passport photographs. You are also required to obtain a French licence if you commit a driving offence and receive penalty points, and/or a restriction on your entitlement to drive. You can also exchange your UK licence for a French licence at the local *préfecture*.

There are an estimated three million false driving licences in France, many produced in north Africa or the middle east. This is said to be due to the high cost of taking the test, which perhaps explains why the government has reduced the cost of obtaining a licence to one euro from the 1st September 2005 for those under 25. For further information about the driving test and licence, practical tests on the *Code de la Route*, and advice on insurance and purchasing a vehicle see www.permis-online.fr

Those who pass their driving test are granted a provisional licence (*permis probatoire*). This lasts for three years. Holders are only permitted to receive up to six penalty points (rather than the standard 12) before they lose their licence.

Traffic regulations and offences

In 2002 over 7,000 people were killed on French roads – twice that for the UK. Over the last few years the authorities have engaged in serious campaigns to reduce the number of accidents, and the figures have started to fall.

The law now presumes that the records produced by an official automatic radar system are valid, unless the driver can prove otherwise. It is no longer necessary for the prosecuting authorities to produce supporting evidence from a police officer. The number of speed cameras in France is on the increase, with plans to have 1,000 operational by the end of 2005. Details, including the locations of the speed cameras, can be obtained from www.securiteroutiere.equipement.gouv.fr. It is, however, illegal to possess or use a radar detector. You can receive a hefty fine, two penalty points and have your licence suspended for up to three years.

Fines in relation to failure to respect traffic lights and stop signs, and using bus lanes are automatically sent to the person registered on the *carte grise*, who is responsible for paying the fine, unless he can prove that he was not responsible.

A person wishing to contest a fine based on a radar record must issue a complaint, pay a proportion of the fine in advance and give the name and address or driving licence number of the person responsible. He is entitled to a copy of the digital picture taken by the radar, which is free of charge. If the registered owner succeeds in his complaint/appeal then the amount he paid is refunded. If he loses, he faces a 10% surcharge on his fine.

The use of mobile telephones is prohibited while driving. A completely hands-free set is permitted, but headsets are not. For holding or using a mobile telephone the punishment is 3 penalty points. Dangerous parking, driving on an emergency lane, driving with no seat belt or helmet, driving over a continuous white line, changing direction without indicating, overtaking dangerously and driving too close to the vehicle in front all attract 3 points and the possibility of having your licence suspended for up to three years. Under rules introduced in 2005 a driver is responsible for ensuring that all passengers under the age of 18 wear a seat belt, and is liable to a fine of €135 for failing to do this. Children under ten must not travel in the front seat of a vehicle, though this is permitted where all other seats are occupied by children under 10. Within the last few years the law has changed to give pedestrians priority on pedestrian crossings, although few drivers appear to be aware of this!

For speeding, the number of points depends upon how much you are over the limit:

Under 20 kph over: 1
20 – less than 30 over: 2
30 – less than 40 over: 3
40 and above: 4

All speeding offences can result in a hefty fine, depending upon the circumstances. For speeds of 30kph or more above the speed limit, you can have your licence suspended for up to three years.

SPEED LIMITS km/h

	normal conditions	rain/snow	visibility less than 50m
Autoroutes:	130	110	50
Dual carriageway	110	100	50
Other roads	90	90	50
Built up areas	50	50	50

50 km/h is just over 31 mph

Drink driving

For drink driving (i.e. a blood / alcohol reading from 0.5 g/l to under 0.8 g/l, and a breath / alcohol reading of 0.25 mg/l to under 0.4 mg/l) there is a steep fine, six penalty points, and a suspension of your licence for up to three years. Those with a blood / alcohol level of 0.8 g/l, or a breath / alcohol level of 0.4mg/l and above face a fine of up to €4,500, 6 penalty points, a three years suspension and a sentence of imprisonment up to two years. In either case a police officer can temporarily confiscate the driver's licence. Similar penalties apply for driving under the influence of drugs. The court has the power to confiscate the driver's vehicle, although it cannot do this and impose a fine or sentence of imprisonment. Any driver responsible for an accident who is found to have been drinking will not be covered for injury to himself or his vehicle, and will face large increases in his insurance premium if and when he is permitted to resume driving.

Accidents causing injuries

Note that *all* accidents resulting in death or injury by careless driving can now result in a prison sentence of up to 5 years. The sentence is 10 years where there are aggravating circumstances such as failing to report, driving under the influence of alcohol or drugs, and driving at 50 kph or more above the speed limit.

Obligations to stop, and also to assist others

Note that if you are the first on the scene of an accident the law requires that you must stop and assist those in difficulty. Failure to assist those in danger is a crime that carries severe penalties. It is for this reason that criminals sometimes pretend to have been the victim of the accident, in order to persuade drivers to stop their car, whereupon they steal from the occupants. For the emergency services telephone 15, for the gendarmerie 17, for fire service 18. If you are using a portable one number covers all three services: 112.

If you are involved in an accident, even in a minor way, the law requires you to stop. Failure to do so, or failure to make your identity known is a serious offence (*un délit de fuite*)

Enforcement of fines and penalties

On a UK initiative the EU has now agreed that member states will enforce each other's orders for fines and penalties. This applies not only to motoring offences but to all legal judgments and fines. Remember that with parking fines and other minor offences, the fine is generally much lower if paid immediately or within seven days.

Traffic information

The French web site www.bison-fute.equipement.fr has a wealth of information, including on road works and congestion. There is a travel bulletin, with a version in English.

Copes of the *Code de la Route* cost about €15 and are published by Codes Rousseau.

Chapter Twelve

FRENCH INHERITANCE LAWS AND THE TAXATION OF CAPITAL

When you become resident in another country you *must* give consideration to the effect that this is likely to have on the passing of your estate, and in particular how it will affect your spouse and children. Especially if you own a business or a property, whether in the UK or France, you really need to take legal advice from a lawyer with knowledge of the law in *both* the UK and France, and taking into account your particular circumstances and testamentary intentions.

French rules of succession

In France, as in other continental European countries, succession law restricts your freedom to dispose of your estate on your death. In brief, if your property is subject to French succession rules, you are obliged to leave a proportion of your estate to your children. Illegitimate and adopted children generally having the same rights of inheritance as the deceased's own legitimate children. If you are domiciled in France, French succession law will apply to all your assets in France, and all your *moveable* assets outside France. *Moveable* assets are all assets, except for land and property, but including shares in a company that owns land and property.

Distribution of your estate: where there is no will

Where the deceased is unmarried at the date of death, his estate is divided equally between his children. Where the deceased is married, the spouse has a choice. He or she can either elect to have a life interest in the whole estate, in which case the children receive the entirety of the estate to divide equally, but only on the death of the surviving spouse. Alternatively she can opt to take an entire interest in a quarter of the estate and is then free to do with this whatever he or she wishes. The remaining three quarters is divided equally between the children. Note that if one or more of the children is not a child from the surviving spouse's marriage with the deceased, then the surviving spouse has no choice – she is obliged to accept a quarter of the estate. There are provisions enabling the spouse and the beneficiaries to realise their interest in the estate, and receive a cash sum. Where there is disagreement, the matter is determined by the courts.

If the deceased dies without descendants, but his parents survive him, the spouse receives one half of the estate.

Where, at the date of death, the surviving spouse is living in a principal residence belonging to both partners he or she is entitled to remain in the property without payment for a period of one year. If the property is rented, the rent is paid by the estate. After that year the spouse is still entitled to elect to remain in the property for life, but is required to pay the other beneficiaries a rent. The surviving spouse is free to rent out the property and find accommodation more suitable to his or her needs.

Distribution of your estate: when you have made a will

The deceased is obliged, irrespective of his own wishes, to leave a proportion of his estate to his children. This is referred to as la *réserve héréditaire*. This amounts to one half of the estate in the case of one child, two thirds where there are two children, and three quarters for three or more children. Where an adult child has died leaving children, his children inherit their parent's share.

Where a deceased dies without children, his parents each inherit a quarter of his estate. It is only where the deceased leaves no direct descendants or ascendants that he is *obliged* to leave part of his estate (one quarter) to his spouse.

Recent changes *permit* a person to leave a proportion of their estate to their spouse. This can be up to a maximum of one half if they have one child, one third if they have two children, or one quarter if they have three or more children. Alternatively one can leave the whole of one's estate to a spouse for life, or three quarters for life, with the remaining quarter absolutely. The remainder of the estate is then split between the children in accordance with the rules set out above. Where there are no children of the marriage, a person is still obliged to leave a proportion of his estate to his parents, if alive, but is allowed to leave a higher proportion to a spouse.

One particularly useful source of further information (in French) is the web site of the *avocat* Maître Gibert at www.sos-net.eu.org/success.

Apart from some adjustments over the years, French rules of succession date from Napoleonic times. They have come in for considerable criticism over the last decade, and are presently under review by the French parliament with the intention of allowing greater freedom for people to dispose of their estates as they wish.

Avoiding French rules of succession

There are a number of ways in which you can favour your spouse, including purchasing a property *en tontine*, making life time gifts, taking out a life assurance policy, deciding upon or changing to the most appropriate matrimonial regime (generally *la communauté universelle avec attribution intégrale*). In brief this is a complex area, and anyone with assets should seek professional advice from a competent lawyer who can advise in the light of their particular circumstances.

Unmarried couples

An unmarried partner is in the same position as any other person not related to you. He or she will only inherit if you have made a will, and even then can only receive a limited proportion of your estate after any family members have received their entitlements. The same situation applies to couples that have entered into a PACS. Those living together should nevertheless seriously consider a PACS – the amount of inheritance tax payable on transfers between unmarried couples is high, and there are possible exemptions for those who have entered into a PACS (see below).

Making a French will

A French will can be in the testator's own handwriting and should be signed and dated by him. It should then be deposited with a *notaire* for safekeeping. Preferably, however, it should be prepared by a *notaire* or other lawyer, and signed in front of two *notaires* or a *notaire* and two witnesses. A will can (though need not) include the appointment of executors, and set out the deceased other wishes, for example in relation to funeral arrangements

By virtue of the Hague Convention of 1961, a will is valid if it is signed in accordance with the requirements either of the country in which it is signed or those of the testator's home country. Accordingly, an English person can sign a will in accordance with the formalities of English law — that is, that the will is signed in the presence of two witnesses, who each sign to have attested the will. A witness to a will cannot inherit under the will, nor can a member of his or her family.

You should keep a copy of your will and leave a copy with your lawyer or executor. The most recent will takes complete precedence over previous wills, provided that it indicates clearly that all previous wills are revoked. Under no circumstances use a homemade French (or English) will of the type that you can buy in the high street. Such wills are often unclear and are far more prone to result in protracted and expensive litigation than a will drafted by a competent lawyer.

Inheritance tax

The complexities are such that advice should be sought from an expert. Tax is paid on the net value of the deceased's *worldwide* estate, after deduction of debts and liabilities. There is double taxation relief, so that inheritance tax paid in France is taken into account in calculating liability for UK inheritance tax, and vice versa.

Where spouses own assets jointly, then only the deceased's share of the asset is taken into account. Where a marriage contract provides that a spouse should receive more than half the joint assets, or the entirety of the joint assets where the couple have opted for *la communauté universelle*, these assets are not subject to inheritance tax and are not included in the tax declaration. Payments under a life insurance policy are partially exempt. The first €152,500 is exempt, thereafter all or some of the value of the policy is subject to tax at 20%. How much of the proceeds above €152,500 is taxed depends upon when the policy was taken out, and how old the deceased was when making the payments.

In 2004 the government announced major changes in relation to inheritance tax, essentially the introduction of a general exemption, the effect of which will be to take most French people's estates out of the tax bracket (in 2000 estate duty was paid on over two thirds of the estates of those who died in that year). The average French estate on death is estimated to be at around €100,000.

There is an exemption for the first €50,000 irrespective of how the estate is to be distributed. This is applied after a 20% exemption on the value of a principal residence. There are then exemptions of €76,000 for a surviving spouse (€57,000 for a PACS partner), and €50,000 per child. There is then a sliding scale as follows:

Threshold € (after exemptions)	Children, grand-children parents	Spouse
Less than 7,600	5%	5%
7,600 – 11,400	10%	10%
11,400 – 15,000	15%	10%
15,000 – 30,000	20%	15%
30,000 – 520,000	20%	20%
520,000 – 850,000	30%	30%
850,000 – 1,700,000	35%	35%
Above 1,7000,000	40%	40%

Note that the individual exemptions apply to gifts during lifetime and covers all gifts in a ten year period – accordingly a person is entitled to transfer assets to each child of €50,000 every ten years without incurring any tax liability. The duty on gifts made by persons under the age of 65 is reduced by 50%, and that on gifts made between the ages of 65 and 75 is reduced by 35%.

If the beneficiary has three or more children, his inheritance tax bill is reduced by €610 per child for the third and any subsequent child if he is the spouse, or in direct line to the deceased. For other relationships the tax is reduced by €305 for the third and any subsequent child.

The transfer of a business

Where a business is transferred during the donor's lifetime, or following his death, only 50% of its value is subject to inheritance tax, provided:

- the donor or deceased operated the business for at least two years;
- all the beneficiaries keep the business together for at least six years;
- at least one of the beneficiaries is engaged in the business for at least five years.

There is an exemption also for shares in a business, with similar conditions. However, in order for the beneficiaries to benefit from this exemption, the donor or deceased must have agreed with the beneficiaries and other shareholders, prior to the gift or his death, that they would retain their shares for at least two years.

There are general instalment terms for paying tax due on the transfer or inheritance of a family business. Payment can be deferred for five years, during which the beneficiary pays interest at only 2.05%, and in many cases at only 0.6%. Thereafter the tax is payable in twenty-six monthly instalments over ten years. Various conditions apply in order to benefit from these provisions, including a stipulation that the beneficiary must retain ownership of at least two thirds of the asset which he has inherited until he has paid the final instalment.

Delaying the payment of inheritance tax

It is possible to pay this tax by instalments. For example, where the total inheritance tax on an estate is less than 5% of the total value of the estate payment can be made in two stages, six months apart. Where the tax represents 20% of the value of the estate, payment can be by ten six-monthly instalments over 5 years. For some assets that are not easily realisable, this period can be extended up to 10 years. There is an interest charge for this, currently 2.05%. In some cases it is possible to defer the payment of inheritance tax. The most important example relates to the transfer of a business or shares in a business (see above, under *Transfer of a Business*).

Avoiding French inheritance tax

There are a number of ways in which you can lawfully reduce tax on gifts and inheritance. These include:

- making gifts before you reach the age of 75: there is a 30% reduction in the tax payable if the donor is under 75, and a 50% reduction if under 65;

- paying the inheritance tax due yourself. Illogically, the payment of the tax by the donor is not considered a taxable transfer. Accordingly the tax bill is significantly lower if the donor reduces the amount he gives away but takes responsibility for paying the tax;

- giving or leaving property to someone for life. That person (e.g. a child) receives the income from the asset until his death, but after his death the property passes to the person named in your will (e.g. your grandchild). Full tax is paid on your death, but no tax is payable on the death of your son or daughter, and hence the property has passed down two generations with inheritance tax being paid only once;

- lend money to your children. If, for example, you lend €50,000 to a child that the child invests in assets that increase in capital value, and perhaps even produce an income, ten years later the combined value of the property and the income produced over ten years might be well over €100,000. On your death the amount of the loan will be added to any other assets your child inherits, but the value of the loan for inheritance tax purposes is only the original loan i.e. €50,000, whereas if you had invested the sum yourself with an identical return and left the property and income from it to your child, inheritance tax would be calculated on the basis of an asset worth €100,000. There is a risk that the authorities will consider that the sum advanced was not a true loan, but a gift, and tax it as such, and indeed impose a substantial penalty. The answer is to provide for a modest interest rate to be payable on the loan, which should be gradually repaid by small instalments;

- taking out a life insurance policy. Whilst the proceeds of a life policy are now taxed, *each beneficiary* is entitled to receive the first €152,500 tax-free (i.e. over €600,000 for a spouse and three children). Furthermore, there is a flat rate of 20%, substantially lower than the higher rates of inheritance tax;

- make use of the ten-yearly tax free exemption. Note that for lifetime gifts, the asset is taxed on the basis of its full value, without deducting any liabilities associated with the asset. On the other hand, if the asset, such as a house subject to a mortgage, is owned by a company in which you own the shares, the shares are taxed on the basis of their real value, taking into account the company's liability under the loan;

- leaving much of your estate in a business, for which there is substantial relief both in the amount of tax charged, and the time in which to pay it;

- making lifetime or death transfers to grand-children, taking advantage of the €30,000 exemption per grand-child (€60,000 for a couple). Even gifts above the exemption limit can result in a reduced total "family" inheritance tax as tax is not paid on two transfers i.e. from you to your child, and from your child to his/her child;

- purchasing a property in joint names with your spouse or partner *en tontine*. On your death, the survivor automatically inherits your share of the property, thereby preventing your share from falling into your estate (and being subject to French rules of inheritance), *and* being subject to inheritance tax. For this to be effective, the joint purchasers need to be of a similar age and have a similar life expectancy, and to avoid inheritance tax the parties to the *tontine* must have lived under the same roof up until the death of the first.

If you have assets of significant value you should seek expert advice. In many respects the tax is a tax on the unwary and the unprepared.

Procedure following a death

A tax declaration must be submitted to the authorities (your local *hôtel des impôts*) by the beneficiaries within six months of the death of the deceased. No declaration is required where the property to declare is below €3,000, or €10,000 where the beneficiaries are a spouse or direct line relatives. For estates under these thresholds ask for a *certificat d'hérédité* from your *mairie*. For more substantial estates you will need to contact a *notaire*.

Pause before handling an estate!

Note that in cases where the deceased's debts exceed the value of his assets, the beneficiaries should consider refusing the inheritance in order to avoid taking on the deceased's debts. If you think that this may be the case, you should consult a lawyer as soon as possible and *before* you deal with *any* of the deceased's property in *any* way.

Capital gains tax (*Impôt sur les plus-values*)

There is a flat rate capital gains tax of 16% for EU citizens not resident in France. This applies to profits made on the sale of assets in France, including personal belongings. Residents pay an additional 11% by way of social security contributions. Expenses relating to the acquisition and sale of the asset are deductible. The costs of carrying out restoration work are deductible.

There are exemptions in relation to real estate as follows:

- property that is your main residence at the time of sale (or that was your main residence less than one year prior to the sale) is totally exempt

- any other property that you have owned for at least five years is subject to a sliding scale exemption of 10% per year from the 6th year onwards. The effect is that the sale of the property is totally exempt of capital gains tax after 15 years.

If you are domiciled in France you may also be liable for capital gains made on the sale of assets in the UK and elsewhere, and vice versa for those domiciled in the UK. A double taxation agreement between France and the UK means that you will not have to pay the full tax twice.

You can find further details relating to capital gains tax at www.impot.gouv.fr

Note that those who are resident for tax purposes outside the EU pay capital gains tax of 33.33% on capital gains on the sale of French real estate.

Wealth tax

French wealth tax, or *L'impôt de solidarité sur la Fortune (ISF)* is an annual tax levied on all those with net taxable assets exceeding €732,000 as at the 1st January each year. If you are domiciled in France then the tax covers all your worldwide assets (and liabilities), otherwise only your net French assets are taken into account. Each spouse or partner submits a separate tax declaration, to be submitted by the 15th June each year. Note that a parent's assets includes all the assets of children under 18. The tax covers most assets, including your home, but not business assets.

Bands (indexed linked)

Under €732,000	Nil
732,000 – 1,180,000	0.55%
1,180,000 – 2,339,000	0.75%
2,339,000 – 3,661,000	1%
3,661,000 – 7,017,000	1.3%
7,017,000 – 15,255,000	1.65%
Above 15,255,000	1.8%

Note that the French and UK governments have reached an agreement upon an exemption for UK nationals who have not taken out French citizenship. The exemption applies to assets outside France during their first five years of residency in France. As at the date of writing it appears that the agreement is not yet in force.

USEFUL ADDRESSES

British Embassy
35, rue Faubourg St. Honoré, 75008 Paris Tel: 01.44.51.31.02
Web site: www.amb-grandebretagne.fr

British Consulates
The British Embassy website (see above) has useful information about living and working in France and links to the five consulates:

Paris: 16 bis rue d'Anjou, 75008 Paris Tel: 01.44.51.31.00

Bordeaux: 353, bd du Président Wilson, BP 91, 33073 Bordeaux
Tel: 05.27..22.21.10

Lille: 11, square Dutilleul, 59800 Lille Tel: 03.20.12..82.72

Lyon: 24, rue Childebert, 69288 Lyon Tel: 04.72.77.81.70

Marseille: 24, av du Prado, 13006 Marseille Tel: 04 91157210

British Vice-consulates
There are also vice-consulates in Biarritz (Tel: 05.59.24.21.40); Le Havre (Tel: 02.35.42.27.47); Nantes (Tel: 02.40.63.16.02); Nice (Tel: 04.93.82.53.06); Toulouse (Tel: 05.61.15.02.02)

The vice-consulate for Monaco is at 33 Bd Princesse Charlotte, BP 265 MC 98005 Monaco Cedex. Tel: 00 377 93509966

Irish Embassy
41, rue Rude, 75016 Paris Tel: 01.44.17.67.00

The French Embassy UK
58 Knightsbridge, London SW7 Tel: 0207 235 8080. The Embassy's website www.ambafrance.org.uk has some useful information

L'Institut Français

Queensbury Place, London SW7 2DT Tel: 0207 8342144
(www.francealacarte.org.uk)

In addition to arranging tuition (including telephone classes), there is a multi-media library, newspapers, restaurant and language facilities. French films are regularly shown, and other cultural events are arranged. There are a number of French shops close by, a children's library (tel: 0207 8382144) and the French Bookshop (0207 584 2840).

Centre Français de Londres

61 Chepstow Place, London W2 4TR. (tel 0207 7920337).

There are also French cultural centres in Bath, Bristol, Cambridge, Exeter, Glasgow, Jersey, Milton Keynes, Manchester, Oxford, and York.

General information

The British Council web site (www.britcoun.org/france) is worth a visit.

The *Association France-Grande-Bretagne* has a considerable number of branches. Contact details: 183 Daumesnil, 75012 Paris Tel: 01.55.78.71.71

The British Community Committee (BCC) publishes a directory of British or Franco-British associations in (available from the British Consulate in Paris).

Adapt in France is a voluntary advice organisation primarily for foreigners in the Alpes-Maritimes. It has a resource library and organises numerous workshops. Tel: 04 93653379; www.adaptinfrance.org.uk

Accueil des Villes Françaises (01 47704585) is a voluntary organisation created to welcome those new to an area. Most of its members are French, though it also welcomes foreigners and organises low cost French lessons. There are branches in most main towns and cities. See the website at www.avt-accueil.com which is in French and English

Other helpful websites include: www.franceguide.com (the French Tourist Office), www.the-languedoc-page.com, www.americansinfrance.net, the www.anglo-info.com sites (covering Riviera, Brittany, Normandy, Poitou-Charentes, Provence); www.french-news.com; www.francekeys.com and also www.maville.com.

Banks

Barclays (Around 50 branches) 01 44951380 www.barclays.fr

In 2005 Abbey National France was taken over by BNP PariBas. Many of the English speaking staff at Abbey National France have bee retained by BNP PariBas. See www.ucb-french-mortgage.com

The Woolwich did operate in France, but its operations were taken over by Crédit Immobilier de France.

Business (see also the Chapter 6 "Setting up and running a business in France")

The Franco-British Chamber of Commerce & Industry, 31 rue Boissy d'Anglas, 75008 Paris Tel: 01.53.30.81.30 Web site: www.francobritishchambers.com

www.entreprendre-enfrance.fr - assists in obtaining business finance and subsidies

Churches

There are many Anglican Churches in France, and a small number of Roman Catholic, Scots Kirk, and Baptist churches that hold services in English. Contact details of most churches are available from British Consulates. For Anglican Churches see www.anglicansonline.org.uk

English Bookshops

See under each region

English language newspapers in France

French News, Brussac, 3 chemin La Monzie 24000 Périgueux (tel: 05 53068448). This is a monthly newspaper, with regional and property supplements and a quarterly magazine.

The Riviera Reporter, 56 chemin de Provence, 06250 Mougins Tel: 04 93457719 www.riviera-reporter.com

The Riviera Times tel: 04 93276000 www.rivieratimes.com

Expat web sites

See a good number of web sites with links from the Back in Blighty website www.backinblighty.com (see "expat links").

Financial advisers

Mortgages Overseas Limited www.moltd.co.uk
Tee Financial plc www.teefinancial.com
Crédit Agricole Britline 00 33 2 31 556789 www.britline.com
Siddals International FR 05 56347551 Investment@johnsiddals.co.uk

French Government Internet Sites

Direction Générale des Impôts: www.impots.gouv.fr
Douanes et droit indirects: www.douane.minefi.gouv.fr
DG CCRF: www.dgccrf.minefi.gouv.fr
Trésor Public: www.impots.gouv.fr
Institut National de la Statistique et des Etudes Economiques: www.insee.fr
Commerce Artisanat: www.pme-commerce-artisanat.gouv.fr
Commerce Exterieur: www.dree.org
DRIRE: www.drire.gouv.fr

These web sites enable you not only to obtain information and documents, but also to obtain necessary forms for completion and to make declarations and payments.

Lawyers

Tee France 01279 755200 www.teefrance.co.uk
Fabian Cordiez 0207 748 3031 Cordiez@mailfrance.com
Fauchon & Levy 0207 4300533 f-l@dircon.co.uk
Sean O'Connor 01732 365378 Seanoconnor@aol.com

Learning French

www.europa-pages.co.uk/france/ has a directory of schools, colleges and universities offering French language tuition in France

www.peoplegoingglobal.com/europe/france.htm also has a directory of universities and other establishments where one can study French in France, and access to the Newcomers Club Directory for France

Alliance Française (courses throughout France) 01 45443828

Removal firms

Allied Pickfords 04 92028606
Allied Arthur Pierre www.alliedarthurpierre.com
Britannia Bradshaw International 00 44 1619460809
www.bradshawinternational.com

Compagnie Générale 04 93 724343 www.grospiron.com
Overs International 00 44 1252 343646 04 92 080781

Worldwide Shipping & Air 00 44 23 80633660
Freight Co. www.worldfreight.co.uk

Satellite installers

www.skydigitalfrance.co.uk
www.digiboxfr.com
frenchelp@aol.com tel 05 62670921 (F)
www.susat@co.uk 08454513133 (UK)
European Satellite Installations 02 96866593 (F) 01242 517629 (UK)

Transport

Airlines

Aer Arann 0800 5872324 www.aerarann.ie
Air France 0845 0845 111 www.airfrance.co.uk
Britair 08 20 820820 www.britair.fr
British Airways 0845 773 3377 www.britishairways.com
British European 0870 567 6676 www.flybe.com
BMI Baby 0870 6070 555 www.flybmi.com
easyJet 0870 6000000 www.easyjet.co.uk
Jet 2 www.jet2.co.uk
Ryanair 0870 1569569 www.ryanair.com

Airports

A comprehensive list of the 143 French airports with links to each of them is
accessible via: www.aeroports.fr

Ferries

Brittany Ferries 0870 556 1600 www.brittany-ferries.com
Condor 0845 345 2000 www.condorferries.co.uk
Hoverspeed 0870 524 0241 www.hoverspeed.com
Irish Ferries 0870 517 1717 www.irishferries.ie
Norfolkline 0870 870 1020 www.norfolkline.com
P & O Ferries 0870 600 0600 www.posl.com
P & O Portsmouth 0870 242 4999 www.poportsmouth.com
Sea France 0870 571 1711 www.seafrance.com
Transmanche 0800 9171201 www.transmancheferries.com

Ferries to Corsica
Corsica Ferries 00 33 825095095 www.corsica-ferries.co.uk
SNCM 0891 702802 www.sncm.fr

Rail
www.raileurope.co.uk 0870 5848848
www.frenchmotorail.com 0870 2415415
www.eurotunnel.com 0870 5353535

Road and Route Planning
www.theaa.com
www.rac.co.uk
www.michelin-travel.com
www.mappy.com

YELLOW PAGES
www.pagesjaunes.fr

DIRECT FLIGHTS TO FRANCE

Note that services are constantly changing and you will need to confirm the up to date position with the particular airline.

FROM UK	TO	AIRLINE
Belfast	Geneva	easyJet
	Nice	easyJet
	Paris	easyJet
Birmingham	Basel-Mulhouse	Swiss, Flybe
	Bergerac	Flybe
	Berne (Switzerland)	Flybe
	Brest	Flybe
	Chambery	Flybe
	Geneva	Flybe
	La Rochelle	Flybe
	Paris	BA, Air France
	Perpignan	Flybe
	Toulouse	Flybe
	Zurich	Swiss
Bournemouth	Lyon	Thomsonfly
	Paris	Thomsonfly
Bristol	Bergerac	Flybe
	Bordeaux	Flybe
	Geneva	easyJet
	Nice	easyJet
	Paris	BA
	Toulouse	Flybe

Coventry	Lyon	Thomsonfly
	Paris	Thomsfly
Doncaster/Sheffield	Lyon	Thomsonfly
	Paris	Thomsonfly
Durham Tees Valley	Paris	BMI Baby
Edinburgh	Geneva	Globespan
	Nice	Globespan
	Paris	BA
Exeter	Brest	Flybe
	Chambery	Flybe
	Geneva	Flybe
	Paris	Flybe
Glasgow	Paris (Beauvais)	Ryanair
Leeds/Bradford	Chambery	Jet2
	Geneva	Jet2
	Nice	Jet2, BMI
	Paris	Jet2, BMI
Liverpool	Basel-Mulhouse	easyJet
	Bergerac	Ryanair
	Carcassonne	Ryanair
	Geneva	easyJet
	Limoges	Ryanair
	Nice	easyJet
	Nimes	Ryanair
	Paris	easyJet
London City	Basel-Mulhouse	Swiss
	Geneva	Swiss, BA
	Paris	Air France
	Zurich	Swiss
London Gatwick	Bordeaux	BA
	Corsica, Bastia	GB Airways
	Geneva	easyJet, BA

	Grenoble	easyJet
	Marseille	easyJet, BA
	Montpellier	BA/GB Airways
	Nantes	Air France, BA/GB Airways
	Nice	BA, easyJet
	Strasbourg	Air France, Britair
	Toulouse	BA, easyJet
	Zurich	BA
London Heathrow	Basel-Mulhouse	BA
	Geneva	BA, Swiss
	Lyon	BA, Air France
	Nice	BA, BMI
	Paris	BA, BMI
	Zurich	BA, Swiss
London Luton	Basel-Mulhouse	easyJet
	Dinard	Ryanair
	Geneva	easyJet
	Grenoble	easyJet
	Lorient	Aer Arann
	Nice	easjyet
	Nîmes	Ryanair
	Paris	easyJet
London Stansted	Basel-Mulhouse	easyJet
	Bergerac	Ryanair
	Biarritz	Ryanair
	Carcassonne	Ryanair
	Dinard	Ryanair
	Grenoble	Ryanair
	La Rochelle	Ryanair
	Lyon	easyJet
	Montpellier	Ryanair
	Nice	easyJet
	Nîmes	Ryanair
	Pau	Ryanair
	Perpignan	Ryanair
	Poitiers	Ryanair
	Rodez	Ryanair
	St. Etienne	Ryanair
	Tours	Ryanair

Manchester	Basel-Mulhouse	Swiss
	Chambery	Jet2
	Geneva	Jet2
	Nice	BA, Jet2
	Paris	BA
	Toulouse	BMI
	Zurich	BA
Newcastle	Geneva	easyJet
	Nice	easyJet
	Paris	easyJet
Norwich	Chambery	Flybe
	Geneva	Flybe
Nottingham /East Midlands	Geneva	easyJet
	Nice	BMI
	Paris	BMI
Southampton	Bergerac	Flybe
	Berne (Switzerland)	Flybe
	Bordeaux	Flybe
	Brest	Flybe
	Chambery	Flybe
	Cherborg	Flybe
	Geneva	Flybe
	La Rochelle	Flybe
	Limoges	Flybe
	Paris	Britair / Air France
	Perpignan	Flybe
	Rennes	Flybe

USEFUL FRENCH WORDS

Jobs and employment

l'ancienneté	length of service
une annonce	advertisement
le bulletin de paie	payslip
le charge de travail	workload
le chef du personnel	personnel manager
une connaissance approfondie	in-depth knowledge
dans l'attente de votre réponse	I look forward to hearing from you
décliner un offre	to decline an offer
un emploi	a job
un employé à temps partiel	part-time employee
un entretien	interview
une enveloppe affranchie avec adresse	stamped addressed envelope
la formation	training
un formulaire de candidature	application form
les frais de déménagement	relocation expenses
les heures supplémentaires	overtime
une lettre manuscrite	hand-written letter
licencier	to dismiss
le licenciement abusif	unfair dismissal
la main-d'oeuvre	workforce
maîtriser quelquechose	to have a good `command of
perfectionner mes connaissances du français	to perfect my French
un poste	a position
poser sa candidature	to apply
le profil du poste	job description
promouvoir	to promote
recommander quelqu'un	to recommend someone
recruter	to recruit
des renseignements plus complets	further information
un répondant	referee
le salaire actuel	current salary
le salaire de base	basic wage

le syndicat	trade union
un système de primes	incentive scheme
le travail au noir	moonlighting
travailler à son compte	to work freelance

In the office

un agrandissement	enlargement
une agrafe	staple
le bureau paysager	open plan office
un circulaire	circular
classer	to file
un classeur à anneaux	ring binder
le clavier	keyboard
le console de visualisation	VDU (visual display unit)
le courrier électronique	electronic mail
le destructeur de documents	shredder
dicter	to dictate
la disquette	floppy disk
le dossier	file
un double	duplicate
l'écran	screen
une fiche de transmission	compliments slip
une imprimante	printer
un listing	print out
le materiel de bureau	office equipment
le numéro de poste	extension number
l'ordre du jour	agenda
le perforateur	punch
le personnel administratif	clerical personnel
le poste de travail	workstation
la télécopie	fax
le traitement de données	data processing
le trombone	paper clip
Qui est à l'appareil?	Who's speaking?
Ne quittez pas	Hold the line
transmettre un message	to take a message
Je vous rappelle	I'll call you back
Je vous le passe	I'm putting you through

Renting

le bail	a lease
le bailleur	lessor (the owner of a tenanted property)
la caution	guarantee or security deposit
le congé	notice of termination
le contrat de bail	rental contract
la durée	duration
un Etat des Lieux	record of condition of property at start and end of tenancy
les honoraries	fee / commission of agent
le loyer	rent
le préavis	notice
le propriétaire	landlord
le renouvellement	renewal of lease
les travaux	building works
un voisin de palier	a neighbour on the same floor

Utilities

un abonnement	standing charge
le compteur	meter
EDF/GDF	Electricité de France/Gaz de France
le gaz de ville	mains gas
la puissance	electricity power rating
le relevé	reading (of a meter)

Financial

arriver à l'échéance	to fall for renewal / to expire
un banque	bank
une Caisse d'Epargne	savings bank
le compte courant	current account
le comptable	accountant
un compte d'epargne	savings account
constituer une société	to form a company
le découvert	overdraft
un distributeur de billets	cash machine
un droit	a right
le droit de succession	inheritance tax
encaisser un chèque	to cash a cheque
un emprunt	loan
exempt d'impôts	tax free
faire faillite	to go bankrupt
le forfait	fixed amount or all in price

les frais de banque	bank charges
les frais de dossier	mortgage arrangement fee by bank
l'hypothèque	mortgage
le guichet	counter
HT = hors taxe	excluding tax
TTC = toutes taxes comprises	including tax
un huissier	official legal officer whose duties include those of a bailiff in the UK
la location-vente	hire-purchase
le montant	total to be paid
le numéro d'agence	sort code
une opération	transaction
payer en espèces	to pay in cash
payer en liquide	to pay in cash
la plus-value	capital gain
le prélèvement	direct debit
le prêt	loan
un prix à forfait	all in one price
le relevé de compte	statement
le retrait éclair	a withdrawal from a cash dispenser
retirer de l'argent	to withdraw money
le RIB = relevé d'identité bancaire	bank account details
une société	company
SARL = société à responsabilité limitée	limited company
SCI = société civile immobilière	non-trading property company
le solde	balance
la tacite reconduction	automatic renewal of contract
le taux d'échange	exchange rate
le taux d'intérêt	rate of interest
le taxe d'habitation	local tax on occupation of property
le taux effectif global (TEG)	annual percentage rate (APR)
la taxe foncière	local tax on ownership of property
le transfert électronique de fonds	electronic funds transfer
TVA = taxe sur la valeur ajoutée	VAT
un versement	deposit

Medical

ausculter quelqu'un	to listen to someone's heart and lungs
une brûlure	burn
le cabinet	doctor's surgery
un carnet de santé	medical records book held by patient

la carte vitale	medical card for automatic reimbursement
une contusion	bruise
le coup de soleil	sunburn
la formule de consentement	consent form
être à jeun	to have eaten or drunk nothing
l'insolation	sunburn
une ordonnance	prescription
un médecin conventionné	doctor who works within the French health service
un médecin généraliste	GP
un oto-rhino-laryngologiste	ENT surgeon
le passé médical	medical history
une pharmacie de garde	duty chemist
le pouls (pronounced "pou")	pulse
une radio	X-ray
le sparadrap	elastoplast
la rage des dents	raging toothache
tâter le pouls de quelqu'un	to take somone's pulse
un rhume	a cold
le SAMU (Service d'Aide Médicale d'Urgence)	emergency medical service
le torticolis	whiplash

Dealings with officialdom

atteindre sa majorité	to come of age
c'est capital	its essential
ce n'est pas de notre resort	it is not our responsibilty
la citoyennété	citizenship
un conjoint	spouse
contourner une loi	to get round a law
un contribuable	taxpayer
la déclaration des revenus	tax declaration
un dégrèvement	reduction, abatement, tax allowance
un délit	a wrong
le dossier	file
la double nationalité	dual nationality
une erreur de bonne foi	genuine mistake
une fausse affirmation	false statement
le Fisc	income tax authorities
l'hôtel des impôts	tax office
un manquement à une obligation	breach of a duty
mettre en question	to call into question

la résidence effective	actual residence
être de bonne vie et moeurs	to be of good character
être par écrit	to be in writing
une carte de séjour	residence permit
un intermédiaire	agent
un oubli	an oversight
les personnes à charge	dependants
remplir	to fill out (a form)
réparer un oubli	to rectify an omission
le commissariat de police	police station
la Mairie	town hall
un impôt	tax
obtempérer	to obey, comply with
recevoir / toucher des subventions	to receive a grant
respecter	to comply with
être interprété comme	to be construed as
la subvention	subsidy, grant

Internet

l'adresse e-mail	e mail address
l'arabas (the "s" is pronounced)	@
une copie cachée	blind copy (bcc)
l'écran	screen
un e-mail	e-mail
faire suivre	to forward
le fichier	file
un fichier joint	attachment
un lien	link
le logiciel	software
la mot de passe	password
la moteur de recherche	search engine
le point-com	dotcom
les outils	tools
précédent	previous/back
quitter	exit
rédiger un courrier	to send an e-mail
le réseau	network
télécharger	to download
le site internet	website
suivant	next
le tiret	hyphen

Internet abbreviations

@+	*à plus tard* / see you later
@2m1	*à demain* / see you tomorrow
cpg	*c'est pas grave* / no matter
dsl	*désolé* / sorry
JMS	*jamais* / never
mr6	*merci* / thank you
p2k	*pas de quoi* / you're welcome
TOQP	*t'es occupé?* / are you busy?

You and your car

l'aire de stationnement	parking area
l'aire de service	parking area with petrol station, restaurant, hotel
l'angle mort	blind spot
l'avertisseur sonore / klaxon	horn
la bande cyclable	cycle lane
la batterie car	battery
la boîte de vitesse	gear box
la borne d'appel d'urgence	emergency call box
la bretelle d'accès	slip road, motorway access road
le carrefour à sens giratoire / rondpoint	roundabout
la carte grise	registration document
cédez le passage	give way
la ceinture de sécurité	seat belt
clignoter	to indicate
le coffre	boot
le conducteur	driver
le cône	traffic cone
le constat amiable	accident report form to be signed by both parties
la crevaison	puncture
dépasser / doubler	to overtake
déraper	to skid
la distance de freinage	braking distance
la distance de réaction	reaction distance
l'essuie-glace	windscreen wiper
les feux tricolores / feux	traffic lights
les feux	headlights
les feux de détresse	hazard lights
le frein principal / frein à pied	brakes
le frein de parcage / frein à main	handbrake

la fuite	leak
le gonflage	air (for tyres)
l'huile	oil
une infraction pénale	a criminal offence
les intempéries	bad weather
la marche arrière	reversing
le numéro minéralogique /	
d'immatriculation	car registration number
le panneau	signpost
le passage pour piétons	pedestrian crossing
le pare-brise	windscreen
le péage	toll
percuter	to crash into
porter secours à	to rescue, come to the aid of
la portière	car door
la remorque	towing; trailer
le rétroviseur	car mirror
la roue de secours	spare wheel
les secours	emergency services
sens interdit	no entry
le siège	car seat
le témoin	witness
tomber en panne	to breakdown
les travaux	roadworks
verbaliser quelqu'un	to charge someone
la vitesse	speed
les zébras	hatched lines (no go areas)

CLOTHES' SIZES

Women (coats, dresses, skirts)

UK	8	10	12	14	16	18	20	22
US	6	8	10	12	14	16	18	20
France	34	36	38	40	42	44	46	48

Women (blouses and jumpers)

UK	31	32	34	36	38	40	42	(inches)
US	6	8	10	12	14	16	18	(size)
France	81	84	87	90	93	96	99	(cm)

Women (shoes)

UK	3.5	4/4.5	5	5.5	6	6.5	7
US	5	5.5/6	6.5	7	7.5	8	8.5
France	36	37	38	39	39	40	41

Men (suits)

UK/US	36	38	40	42	44	46	48
France	46	48	50	52	54	56	58

Men (shirts)

UK/US	14	14.5	15	15.5	16	16.5	17	17.5
France	36	37	38	39	41	42	43	44

Men (shoes)

UK	6	7	8	9	10	11	12
US	7	8	9	10	11	12	13
France	39	41	42	43	44	45	46

Children (Clothes)

UK	16/18	20/22	24/26	28/30	32/34	36/38
US	2	4	6	8	10	12
France	92	104	116	128	140	152

Children (Shoes)

UK	2	3	4	4.5	5	6	7	7.5	8	9
US	2	3	4	4.5	5	6	7	7.5	8	9
France	18	19	20	21	22	23	24	25	26	27
UK	10	11	11.5	12	13	1	2	2.5	3	4
US	10	11	11.5	12	13	1	2	2.5	3	4
France	28	29	30	31	32	33	34	35	36	37

PUBLIC HOLIDAYS

1st January

Easter Sunday and Easter Monday
1st May
8th May

Ascension Day (sixth Thursday after Easter)

14th July (Bastille Day)

15th August

1st November

11th November

25th December

FURTHER READING

Biggins, Alan (2002) *Selling French Dreams*, Kirkdale Books

Brame, Geneviève (2004) *Chez vous en France*, Kogan Page

Davey, Charles (2005) *The Complete Guide to Buying Property in France*, Kogan Page

Davey, Charles (expected publication 2006) *Living on the Riviera* Howtobooks

Hart, Alan (2004) *Going to Live in Paris* Howtobooks

Hunt, Deborah (2003) *Starting and Running a B&B in France*, Howtobooks

Mayle, Peter (2000) *A Year in Provence*, Penguin

Nadeau, Jean-Benoit & Barlow, Julie (2004) *Sixty Million French People Can't Be Wrong. What makes the French so French?* Robson Books

Platt, Polly (2003) *French or Foe?* Cultural Crossings Limited

INDEX

Buy French property with confidence!

Anticipate potential problems and avoid expensive mistakes with our expert legal guidance and in-depth knowledge.

We will:

- Liaise directly with the vendor or agent and the notaires, and check all documentation to ensure there are no unwelcome surprises.

- Guide you through the maze of French property law and protect your financial interests with respect to inheritance, wills and tax.

- Keep you fully informed with 24-hour on-line updates on the progress of your purchase.

- Offer you a fixed price package at highly competitive rates.

We can also offer advice on financing your purchase through our associate company, Mortgage Overseas Limited. www.moltd.co.uk
Charles Davey, the author of this guide, is a consultant to Tee France.

 TEE FRANCE

Tee France
Stanley Tee
High Street Bishop's Stortford
Hertfordshire CM23 2LU
England
00 44 (0)1279 755200
www.teefrance.co.uk

...ited is not a firm of solicitors. It is a separate business in which the partners of Stanley
...Tee France is a division of Stanley Tee.

STANLEY FEE

Mortgage Overseas Limited.
tee have a financial interest.